The Sensory Child *Gets Organized*

Proven Systems for Rigid, Anxious, or Distracted Kids

Carolyn Dalgliesh

A Touchstone Book
Published by Simon & Schuster
New York London Toronto Sydney New Delhi

This publication contains the opinions and ideas of its author. It is intended to provide helpful and informative material on the subjects addressed in the publication. It is sold with the understanding that the author and publisher are not engaged in rendering medical, health, or any other kind of personal professional services in the book. The reader should consult his or her medical, health, or other competent professional before adopting any of the suggestions in the book or drawing inferences from it.

The author and the publisher specifically disclaim all responsibility for any liability, loss, or risk, personal or otherwise, which is incurred as a consequence, directly or indirectly, of the use and application of any of the contents of this book.

The names and identifying characterstics of the children and families mentioned in this book have been changed.

Touchstone
A Division of Simon & Schuster, Inc.
1230 Avenue of the Americas
New York, NY 10020

Copyright © 2013 by Carolyn Dalgliesh

All rights reserved, including the right to reproduce this book or portions thereof in any form whatsoever. For information address Touchstone Subsidiary Rights Department, 1230 Avenue of the Americas, New York, NY 10020.

First Touchstone trade paperback edition September 2013

TOUCHSTONE and colophon are registered trademarks of Simon & Schuster, Inc.

For information about special discounts for bulk purchases, please contact Simon & Schuster Special Sales at 1-866-506-1949 or business@simonandschuster.com.

The Simon & Schuster Speakers Bureau can bring authors to your live event. For more information or to book an event contact the Simon & Schuster Speakers Bureau at 1-866-248-3049 or visit our website at www.simonspeakers.com.

Designed by Ruth Lee-Mui

Manufactured in the United States of America

1 3 5 7 9 10 8 6 4 2

Library of Congress Cataloging-in-Publication Data

Dalgliesh, Carolyn.
The sensory child gets organized : proven systems for rigid, anxious, or distracted kids / by Carolyn Dalgliesh.—
First Touchstone trade paperback edition.
pages cm
1. Parents of exceptional children. 2. Parents of children with disabilities. 3. Orderliness. I. Title.
HQ759.913D35 2013
648'.8—dc23 2013015661

ISBN 978-1-4516-6428-7
ISBN 978-1-4516-6429-4 (ebook)

To Ian for his courage, to Ella for her strength,
and to Ron for his unwavering support.

I ♥ U

Praise for *The Sensory Child Gets Organized*

"A brilliant book. From the opening paragraph and throughout, you know you are in the hands of a master tactician, an expert who knows her stuff cold, and a loving parent who's been there and back. Hugely practical, chock-full of pearls, and written with sweet tenderness, Dalgliesh's book immediately becomes the go-to book on the subject."

—Edward Hallowell, M.D., author of *The Childhood Roots of Adult Happiness* and coauthor of *Driven to Distraction*

"Open this book and read a description of a well-regulated, efficient, effective child going through the day. Imagine—this organized child can be yours! Employing Carolyn Dalgliesh's sensible systems for sensory kids, you will easily learn to help your child get in sync, at home and in the world."

—Carol Kranowitz, author of *The Out-of-Sync Child*

"Carolyn Dalgliesh has skillfully identified techniques, strategies, and practical organizing solutions that will provide these children—and their families—the much needed structure, peace, and calm they need. *The Sensory Child Gets Organized* will enable parents to better deal with their child's challenging sensory behavior and connect more deeply with those we love the most—our children."

—Peter Walsh, *New York Times* bestselling author of *It's All Too Much* and *Does This Clutter Make My Butt Look Fat?*

"Kids with SPD live in a chaotic world paved with bumps at every turn that sabotages their efforts to do ordinary tasks needed to succeed in the world and creates on-going frustration, failure, distress, and anxiety. Carolyn Dalgliesh's well organized and easy to follow book offers strategies to greatly help smooth out their path so these kids can navigate their day to day world more smoothly and successfully."

—Sharon Heller, Ph.D., author of *Too Loud, Too Bright, Too Fast, Too Tight*

"Carolyn Dalgliesh provides an insightful, creative, and most positive look at a child with sensory processing disorder. This work will soon be a 'go-to' book to learn how to support this very sensitive, delicate, and often gifted child."

—Elaine Hall, author of *Seven Keys to Unlock Autism* and founder of The Miracle Project

"Sure, Dalgliesh covers organization with checklists and labeled bins. But this book goes much further! 'Organizing' in this book means giving parents the techniques to meet the challenges that are unraveling their special needs child. Abounds in excellent, practical, and empathic strategies to help a child organize his/her mindset and thrive."

—Martin L. Kutscher, M.D., pediatric neurologist and author of *Kids in the Syndrome Mix of ADHD, LD, Asperger's, Tourette's, Bipolar and More!*

"Carolyn Dalgliesh created a rich resource for both parents and professionals supporting individuals with sensory challenges. She braids her organizing expertise with evidenced-based practices to give the reader a road map on how to help their child be more successful at home, at school, and in the community. Her proven systems are easy to understand and to set up. I think parents and professionals alike will find many important strategies in this book for their children, students, or themselves!"

—Joanne G. Quinn, executive director of The Autism Project

"An amazing resource for families with children with a variety of diagnoses who have sensory challenges. . . . As she aptly suggests, one of the great secrets to success with sensory kids is purposeful organization. . . . [T]his book provides solutions that will be of use to all parents of children with sensory challenges."

—Lucy Jane Miller Ph.D., director of STAR (Sensory Therapies And Research) Center and author of *Sensational Kids* and *No Longer a Secret*

"[B]ridges the gap between therapeutic support and practical organizational strategies by guiding the parent . . . with compassionate, solution-oriented techniques. Carolyn's book is a must for any parent who is tired of nagging and wishes to help their child become self-reliant."

—Sandy Maynard, AD/HD expert and founder of Catalytic Coaching

"Carolyn Dalgliesh offers us a clear picture of the many behaviors exhibited by children with sensory issues, more importantly she offers practical suggestions and systems parents can use while helping their child succeed in school and life. Keep this book close at hand; you will refer to it often."

—Donna Goldberg, author of *The Organized Student*

"*The Sensory Child Gets Organized* includes a breadth of strategies covering the routine (e.g., morning schedule) to the not-so-routine (e.g., the family vacation) . . . readers will find relatable examples and realistic advice for implementation for these events and everything in between. Carolyn's passion for sensory organizing is clear throughout the book. It is apparent that she lives by these principles, personally and professionally, and that they have revolutionized her life and the lives of her clients."

—Amy Laurent, educational consultant, coauthor of the SCERTS Model

"Packed with superb strategies for creating calming sensory spaces, reassuring routines and checklists, organizing overwhelming environments, and more, this is a sensational book for helping kids with sensory challenges to feel and function better every day."

—Lindsey Biel, OTR/L, coauthor of *Raising a Sensory Smart Child*

Contents

Part 1

Understanding Your Sensory Child

Chapter 1

How Sensory Organizing Worked for Me

Sensory Kids Need Special Solutions

Imagine your mornings at home with your child running more peacefully. You knock on the door, ask him to get dressed, and head down to the kitchen. He selects a shirt from one bin, jeans from another, and has time to run downstairs and enjoy a quick breakfast. When it's time to head out the door, he grabs his backpack (packed the night before) from his backpack hook, grabs his shoes that are waiting in his shoe bin, and leaves for school.

In the afternoon, he comes home, has a snack, and pulls out a homework plan sheet that helps him map out a homework time/break time schedule. After getting through some of the hardest homework, he takes a planned fifteen-minute break in his room playing with his action figures. At dinnertime, he is able to engage in conversation and stay seated by playing dinner conversation games. After dinner, he runs seamlessly through the evening routine of a chore, finishing homework, packing his backpack, and enjoying some free time, finally making the transition to bedtime relaxing and calm.

If you are supporting a rigid, anxious, or distracted child, this scenario might seem like a fairy tale. I'm here to tell you, as a professional organizer and as the parent of a sensory child, that this can be your reality. It's all about learning how to tap into simple systems, routines, and visual guides to support and organize your sensory child: tools that can empower both your child and your entire family.

The numbers are staggering: thousands of young children are being diagnosed each year with anxiety disorder, attention-deficit/hyperactivity disorder (AD/HD), autism spectrum disorders (autistic disorder, Asperger's disorder, pervasive developmental disorder–not otherwise specified or PDD-NOS), pediatric bipolar or mood disorder, obsessive-compulsive disorder (OCD), or sensory processing disorder (a behavior profile commonly seen with kids who have these diagnoses). There is also increasing evidence that some environmental factors like Lyme disease and PANDAS (pediatric autoimmune neuropsychiatric disorders associated with strep) can trigger or exacerbate some of these neurological and behavioral challenges.

The treatment options for kids who present with these types of sensory issues are vast. Much success can come from a combination of supports such as speech therapy, occupational therapy, behavioral therapy, accommodations/supports at school, and medication. However, there is so much that you as a parent can do, as well. That's where this book comes in. As a parent, how do you learn how to support your "sensory" child in the home and make your day-to-day living experience less stressful and more meaningful?

"Sensory" kids—including those with AD/HD, anxiety disorder, OCD, sensory processing disorder, bipolar disorder, and autism—often look at the world through a different lens. There are so many questions parents have when learning to live with and support these sensory kids.

- How can you develop simple ways to communicate and connect with your child?
- How can you learn to anticipate and deal with the seemingly simple activities that create a major challenge for your child?
- How can you create spaces in your home to help your sensory child feel comfortable and at ease?

These are the kinds of practical, everyday issues that your doctors or therapists might not address. That's why I wrote *The Sensory Child Gets*

Organized: to help bridge the gap between essential clinical support and practical in-home solutions.

Through my experience as the parent of a sensory child and as a professional organizer, I know that sensory kids need special organizing solutions. Parents want to connect with their children, want to learn their "language," and have peace at home. These Sensory Organizing techniques will show you how to use simple organization, structure, and visual aids in your everyday life to address some of your child's challenging sensory behaviors. This book offers practical, easy-to-implement strategies that can be life changing for you, your sensory child, and your entire family. Our sensory kids are smart, perceptive, connected, and loving when they feel understood and supported, and this is our goal!

My Journey to Systems for Sensory Kids

My journey into the world of sensory kids and Sensory Organizing began in 2002, as my husband and I were learning how to live with and support our own sensory child. For our son, who was born healthy and happy, things seemed to take a sudden turn between eighteen months and two years of age. He started to show signs of some developmental delays, such as regression in speech and a new hyperfocus on certain activities and repetitive play. He also had explosive episodes, became overwhelmed with playgroups, and seemed to be much more internally focused. We then began the sometimes-frustrating process of evaluations, reports, and appointments trying to get a diagnosis. We were looking for answers. What is happening to our child?

At age two, our son began getting speech and occupational therapy support through Early Intervention. It was extremely helpful for some very specific tasks that were challenging for our son and gave him some critical sensory input that he needed. I remember being so overwhelmed with all the other difficulties during our day: getting him to take a bath, cutting his nails, preparing him for a change in schedule, getting him to sit through dinner, and taking him to a birthday party, just to name a few. Many seemingly simple tasks were anything but simple. I was continually bombarding our speech and occupational therapists for information about how to support the way he was seeing the world, and how to make the days run more smoothly for him and for our new daughter, who arrived when he was two years old.

Our son was like many children whose presentation comes down to "a little bit of everything." Because his symptoms present as a combination of many diagnoses, I developed a real appreciation for what families were living with when supporting sensory processing disorder, AD/HD, anxiety, autism spectrum disorder, Asperger's disorder, mood disorders, as well as strep-triggered tics and obsessive-compulsive disorder (PANDAS), and neurological symptoms (including attention problems, short-term memory loss, depression, mood swings, and/or learning disabilities) as a result of late-stage Lyme disease. I also began to develop a few key concepts to help my son deal with some of the challenges he faced, such as getting ready for school in the morning or doing homework in the evening.

Over time, I began to see the power of structure and routine for my son in helping him navigate his day. He was a visual learner (like many sensory kids) and we began to tap into visual supports to help him with simple tasks inside the home. When we gave him labeled clothes storage bins, he was able to put clothes away and pick out clothes for school independently and without frustration. This became life changing for us. We made a conscious effort to concentrate on what was hard for him, and then develop a system or strategy to support him in overcoming the challenge. By picking a few challenging behaviors at a time and coming up with simple visual supports and routines, we could help him slowly modify his behavior.

I also noticed how helpful it was to have his environment set up in a way that made sense to him. When he had a defined homework space, a visual homework plan with built-in breaks, and graphic organizers for difficult homework, he could be successful. The internal confusion could be countered externally with spaces that were clearly defined, had systems in place, and had visual supports incorporated. The impact of these simple changes was incredible. He slowly began to learn what systems worked well for him and when he needed a plan in place.

The power of structure and routine provided an additional benefit that I had not planned on—it also supported me! The sensory parenting experience for many involves a journey from denial to acceptance that can be a stressful and overwhelming experience, even for the most well-adjusted, typical adults out there. This stress is magnified tremendously if the parent has their own challenges around anxiety, emotional regulation, or distractibility and needs to learn how to help their child manage similar challenges. Sensory Organizing gives us parents the added gift of structure, routines, and visual aids that can support the process of managing life, our executive functioning challenges, and our overwhelmed days. When we support ourselves with simple organization, structure, and routines, we are infinitely better at supporting our sensory kids. Sensory Organizing can truly become a gift for the entire family.

When I started my professional organizing business a few years ago, I knew there would be a piece of this kind of "sensory organizing" involved. Because the need is so great, that "piece" turned into a separate business, and Systems for Sensory Kids (SSK) was born. Recognizing how many overlapping behaviors there are in many different pediatric neurological and behavioral disorders, I wanted to focus on those challenging behaviors that families were living with daily. There is no doubt that these kids are extremely bright and can be very successful in almost anything they do as long as they have a plan in place that supports their way of processing information and sets them up to do well. Success breeds confidence.

The main goal of *The Sensory Child Gets Organized* is to empower you and your family with a few simple, effective techniques that will help you and your child be happier, calmer, and more successful. I am not a doctor or clinician, and I never make a diagnosis. But from my own experience, extensive research, and working with so many other families, I know there is an enormous need for parent-based, practical solutions for the everyday challenges of raising a rigid, anxious, or distracted child. This book gives you a game plan for learning how to live with and best support your sensory kids at home which, in turn, will give them increased self-awareness and confidence. I also believe strongly in the power of a team, and part of the team in supporting most sensory kids is going to be that essential clinical support from psychologists, occupational therapists, speech therapists, pediatricians, neuropsychologists, and the many other professionals who work to support sensory kids. Early, consistent clinical support is so important in helping our kids reach their potential.

The most important team, and the team that will have the biggest impact, is the team at home. Our whole family thrived with these supports, and it has helped us all have a better idea of who we are, what works for us individually, and how we can best support each other.

Let's Empower You to Learn Your Child's Language

I know firsthand the power of learning your child's language and translating that knowledge into tangible supports for everyday life. We know that our sensory kids are bright, creative, and long to be successful in their daily tasks. I will teach you simple ways to learn your sensory child's language, as well as universal approaches to creating visual aids that will support current challenges.

By the end of this book, my goal is to have you seamlessly observing, prioritizing needs, and creating supports for all types of different experiences. Having the correct sensory supports at home, and available for out-of-home experiences, will have a dramatic impact. These tools will also help our sensory kids feel capable, successful, and well on their way to a clear self-awareness of their own strengths.

So let's start learning a new language, educating your team at home, and Sensory Organizing!

Chapter 2

Who Is a "Sensory" Child?

Different Profiles but Common Challenges

One of the special things about sensory kids is that they process the world in a slightly different way. Whereas a typical child is innately able to prepare for and navigate daily life experiences, this can be much more challenging for sensory kids. When we learn to tap into some of their amazing gifts around visual processing, strong connections to specific interests, creative thinking, powerful imaginations, or channeled focus, we can begin to support their unique experiences. If you can figure out how to see the world through their eyes, it can help you be a better advocate for them and help you organize their home environment for greater success.

Sensory kids—those with sensory processing disorder, AD/HD, anxiety disorder, OCD, bipolar disorder, and autism spectrum disorders—come to us with strengths and challenges that can have a unique presentation in each child. On top of this, there are a few diagnoses, including sensory processing disorder, that are considered controversial in the sense that they are not officially recognized by physicians, mental health professionals, health insurance companies, and federal and state special education agencies. This is because a few have not been included in the most recent revision of *Diagnostic and Statistical Manual of Mental Disorders* (DSM-5). This is where the power of Sensory

Organizing comes into play; we will focus much more on the behaviors than on any specific diagnosis. Because when you begin to understand your child's unique symptoms, you can provide tangible supports for your sensory child at home and become a powerful advocate for him or her out in the world. The information and tools in this book will teach you how to do that.

We are going to learn a few things in this chapter that will help us get started down the road to support and advocacy. First, we'll look at some of the common diagnoses that fall under the sensory profiles we aim to support. Next, we'll highlight some of the common factors we see across several diagnoses. Finally, we'll look at some of the overlapping challenges we often see in all types of sensory kids. Developing a solid understanding of different diagnoses as well as common factors and overlapping challenges gives us a road map to get started.

The Sensory Profile: Common Diagnoses

Now it is time to develop a basic understanding of some of the common neurological disorders or quirky challenges that our sensory kids are learning to live with inside and outside the home. It is important to remember that a diagnosis can look very different from child to child. You'll note some of the consistent traits and behaviors in the more common diagnoses, as well as the overlapping challenges you will see in all of these profiles. Each discussion includes a case study of a child exhibiting this diagnosis, so you can get a picture of how it might express itself in a real child.

Sensory Processing Disorder

Sally was a small, timid little girl who just started nursery school. Although she liked arts and crafts, she did not like it if paint or glue got on her hands and would go right to the sink to wash it off. When out in the playground, she would shy away from the swing and the tire tubes, instead choosing to stay near the slide. She sometimes seemed clumsy, and seemed to trip and fall more often than the other kids in her class did. She did not like loud noises and was always plugging her ears when the boys in her class were running around playing tag. Mealtime with Sally was also challenging. She was a picky eater and certain food textures would make her gag and cry. After visits to many specialists, Sally was diagnosed by an occupational therapist with sensory processing disorder.

Sensory processing disorder (SPD) is a diagnosis children can get when they are showing developmental delays or behavioral challenges at very young ages. According to Dr. Lucy Jane Miller in her book *Sensational Kids*, it is estimated that around 1 in 20 kids have SPD.

SPD was first described by Dr. A. Jean Ayres in 1972, and her research helped make the connection between behavior and sensory processing challenges. SPD is defined as a problem in the central nervous system's ability to process information from the senses (movement, hearing, touch, smell, taste, sight). This can affect the way the brain receives and integrates sensory information, making it hard to respond to many different experiences in an appropriate way. SPD can be a standalone disorder, or it can coexist with some of the other disorders we will talk about in this chapter. Like many disorders, the effects of SPD are on a spectrum with some kids experiencing mild challenges and some experiencing major difficulties.

SPD can affect social, learning, and emotional development, attention, coordination, speech and language skills, gross and fine motor development, as well as how kids respond to all types of sensory input from their senses.

Attention-Deficit/Hyperactivity Disorder (AD/HD)

John was a bright, curious boy who could light up a room with his energy. This energy and curiosity, combined with his challenges around paying attention and controlling his impulses (what he called his "gotta do its"), meant that John had a hard time staying on task at school and at home. After asking John to get dressed and come downstairs for breakfast a number of times to no avail, Mom would go upstairs to find John jumping on his bed or playing on the floor of his bedroom still in his PJs. At school, the teacher would have to constantly talk to, redirect, and encourage John to keep him on task. John was constantly moving between the place of excitement where he would blurt out whatever was on his mind with his friends and being withdrawn and frustrated. John was living with AD/HD. (We'll learn more about John and how his family used Sensory Organizing to help him get through his day more smoothly in chapter 9.)

Many sensory kids are living with attention-deficit/hyperactivity disorder. Many of us remember the old categories of ADD: attention-deficit disorder (inattentive diagnosis) and ADHD (attention-deficit/hyperactive disorder (hyperactive and/or combined diagnosis). According to the *DSM-IV,* the diagnosis was listed as AD/HD with three subtypes:

1. AD/HD, predominantly inattentive type,
2. AD/HD, predominantly hyperactive-impulsive type, and
3. AD/HD, combined type

The definition and subtypes of AD/HD may be changed in the DSM-5. A 2012 Centers for Disease Control (CDC) report said that more than 8 percent of kids are diagnosed with AD/HD. This number could be conservative due to misdiagnoses or assigning AD/HD–like behavior as normal behavior for kids. In their book *Driven to Distraction,* Edward M. Hallowell and John J. Ratey describe the challenge of properly diagnosing AD/HD and highlight how important an early diagnosis and treatment are for supporting these kids and helping them (and their families) learn how to live with and embrace the gifts that come along with AD/HD.

In *Taking Charge of ADHD*, Russell Barkley defines this condition as a developmental disorder of self-control that consists of problems with attention span, impulse control, and activity level. According to research, the central problem for most kids with AD/HD is the inability to inhibit or control behavior.

The symptoms of AD/HD can mimic symptoms of some other diagnoses, and though it can be easier to diagnose in some kids with the more classic presentation of hyperactivity and impulsivity, it can be difficult to diagnose when the main symptoms suggest inattention, such as making careless mistakes, having trouble organizing activities, or having difficulty following instructions.

Anxiety Disorders

Mary was an outgoing girl who outwardly appeared to be confident and happy to friends and teachers at school. Yet she would have rough transitions back to school after being on breaks and vacations. When something important (like a presentation or performance) was going on at school, she found it hard to sleep, had stomach aches, and would often be cranky and irritable leading up to the big event. She also worried about new situations and would ask questions incessantly about the new situation, honing in on every detail. Mary's chronic worry impacted her ability to participate at school and to fully enjoy social experiences. Because of her extended periods of constant worry that had a real impact on her functioning, Mary was diagnosed with generalized anxiety disorder (GAD).

Think about a time when you were in a mall or airport and you looked down and realized you did not see your child anywhere around you. Think of the panic, fear, and paralysis that came over you in that moment. Your heart started racing, your breathing become restricted, and your mind immediately went to the worst-case scenario of what happened to your child. Now imagine that you are a child who has these types of responses to simple, routine things that happen regularly. This will give you a real snapshot of how living with anxiety can affect some of our sensory kids.

A healthy, regulated sense of anxiety can be a great tool for our kids when they are checking out the world around them to see what is safe. When this testing turns to worry and becomes a prevalent part of our child's day and/or gets in the way of normal experiences, this points to an unhealthy expression of anxiety. Anxiety disorders are diagnosed in as many as 1 in 8 children. Due to the growing recognition that most anxiety disorders begin in childhood, anxiety disorder diagnoses in children have increased significantly in recent years. In their book, *Your Anxious Child*, John B. Dacey and Lisa B. Fiore describe the eight major categories of anxiety disorder as:

simple phobia
social phobia
agoraphobia (fear of crowds, crowded places)
panic disorder
generalized anxiety disorder (GAD)
separation anxiety
obsessive-compulsive disorder (OCD)
post-traumatic stress disorder (PTSD).

Sometimes, some of the symptoms may overlap, and kids may be experiencing more than one anxiety disorder at a time. In addition to being a primary diagnosis for many kids, anxiety can be a secondary symptom in many of the other neurological disorders affecting our sensory children.

In *Freeing Your Child from Anxiety*, Tamar Chansky points to the core issue for kids living with anxiety as worry being the automatic, first reaction to all situations. Anxiety can affect all parts of a child's day and give rise to intrusive thoughts and actions that compromise his ability to participate and connect to the world.

Autism Spectrum Disorders Including Asperger's Disorder

Mark was a nine-year-old boy who had a fascination with *Star Wars*—he had been obsessed with everything *Star Wars* since he was about four years old. He knew facts about every movie, character, and book and could talk about them at length whenever prompted—sometimes it was all he talked about! Mom had a very hard time pulling him away from *Star Wars* items and it often made transitions difficult. He had a few friends at school who liked *Star Wars*, but they never wanted to talk about it as much as he did, and they began developing other interests as they got older. Teachers at school said Mark seemed to have a hard time talking to other kids, especially if it was about something other than *Star Wars,* and seemed to have a hard time learning some of the social rules that came with being in fourth grade. Mark sometimes used *Star Wars* to remember people or help him make sense of people. When he met someone new, he would use their looks, gestures, and words to match them up to a character. This helped him not be so nervous about meeting someone new and helped him remember them the next time he saw them. Mark has a diagnosis of Asperger's disorder.

Autism spectrum disorders (ASD) are pervasive developmental disorders that affect communication, social interactions, and the presence of repetitive behaviors, interests, or activities. ASD can have a severe presentation as in autistic disorder, a milder presentation as seen in pervasive developmental disorder–not otherwise specified (PDD-NOS), and a higher functioning presentation as seen in Asperger's disorder. And though it affects communication, the main challenges of Asperger's come from limited social skills and obsessive interest in one or two topics.

Currently, 1 in 88 children is diagnosed with an autism spectrum disorder (1 in 54 for boys). For sensory kids living with ASD or Asperger's, life can be very confusing and overwhelming. They contend with restricted interests, challenges with social interactions and social nuances, challenges in recognizing nonverbal cues, and periods of explosive and rigid behaviors. These kids need information presented in a structured and consistent way in order to process lessons and develop critical life skills.

Mood Disorders, Including Pediatric Bipolar Disorder (BD)

Tim was a nine-year-old boy who had a tremendous amount of energy but could be very unpredictable and had a quick temper. According to his parents, he had what seemed to be cyclical changes in his behavior and energy level. He had long periods where he was very "up," very talkative, seemed to think he could do almost anything, and due to his high energy level, had a very hard time sleeping. Then there were periods where he was much more down, with times of extremely explosive behavior. At these times, he seemed to be in an almost constant state of irritability and frustration. He didn't want much to do with friends and didn't seem to like any of his favorite activities. Tim was diagnosed with bipolar disorder.

Historically, bipolar disorder (BD) was seen in adults primarily and the most common age of onset was late teens to early twenties. The diagnosis of bipolar disorder in children and adolescents has increased fortyfold from the mid-1990s to the present and has been diagnosed in children as young as six years old. According to the National Institute of Mental Health (NAMI), statistics taken from the number of children who were seen at psychiatric facilities showed that 7 percent of these children demonstrated symptoms of bipolar disorder. The hallmark of BD in children is extreme mood changes moving between a place of extreme excitement, also called mania, to a place of sadness and depression. Other symptoms include short temper and periods of chronic irritability, grandiose ideas, and decreased need for sleep. Though bipolar disorder can be more serious with early onset in children, carefully monitored medications and different types of therapy can be a tremendous support to kids living with bipolar disorder.

"Little Bit of Everything" Profile

The name speaks for itself! These are the sensory kids who don't fit into one diagnostic profile and show a few symptoms from many different disorders. These kids may go through the first few years of elementary school with a few different diagnoses leaving parents and teachers scratching their heads trying to figure out how to best support this child. These types of sensory kids are going to have challenges in the same areas we talked about above but as a combination of many pieces like anxiety, distractibility, rigidity, and irritability.

The added challenge about these kids is parents don't know what to call the disorder and are often left to squeezing their sensory child into one diagnostic label in order to get accommodations and services from their school district. There can be the feeling of "where do we belong" that can add to the stress and frustration of learning how to support your family and your sensory child.

Environmental Factors: "Acquired" Diagnoses

Our examination of sensory profiles would not be complete without looking at some of the environmental triggers for rigid, anxious, or distracted behaviors. Although they continue to be under-recognized, we will highlight a few of the environmental factors that our sensory kids might have the highest chance of encountering: strep and Lyme disease

PANDAS and Lyme Disease. Katie was a typical eleven-year-old—she did well at school, had friends she enjoyed, and besides having a few issues with her knee over the last year, she loved playing soccer. Then suddenly, things seemed to change for Katie. She began to have problems remembering simple things, seemed to be either irritable all the time or uncharacteristically anxious about unusual things, and she began to develop rigid rules around food and how it needed to be prepared in order for her to eat it. She was falling behind in school, and she lost interest in being with her friends and playing soccer. With the sudden, uncharacteristic change in her personality along with consistent problems with a swollen knee, Katie received a diagnosis of late-stage Lyme disease.

Pediatric Autoimmune Neuropsychiatric Disorders Associated with Strep (PANDAS). According to the National Institutes of Mental Health, pediatric autoimmune neuropsychiatric disorders associated with strep is a term that describes a subset of children who develop or have a worsening of obsessive-compulsive disorder (OCD) and/or tic disorders such as Tourette's disorder, after exposure to strep infections or scarlet fever. Dr. Susan Swedo and Dr. Henrietta Leonard were the first to identify and describe PANDAS in 1998. Children with PANDAS will have a dramatic onset or worsening of symptoms like vocal tics, motor tics, obsessions or compulsions, irritability, separation anxiety, and AD/HD-like symptoms. In PANDAS, it is believed that the antibodies that are produced to fight the strep bacteria also attack the area of the brain that controls behavior and movement, and this gives rise to OCD-like behaviors and/or tics.

The OCD Foundation states on its PANDAS Fact Sheet that strep is not the only immune system disease that can cause a sudden onset of OCD, and the foundation listed other possibilities as Lyme disease, thyroid disease, and lupus among others. While a growing number of parents and clinicians think that PANDAS is a causal factor in sudden onset obsessive-compulsive disorder, PANDAS is not yet widely understood or accepted in the medical community.

Lyme Neuroborreliosis (Neuro-Lyme). According to the CDC, Lyme disease is one of the fastest growing infectious diseases in the country. In 2007, there were more than 27,000 cases of Lyme disease reported to the CDC, but because only a small percentage of cases were reported, it is believed that this number was actually up to ten times higher. The CDC lists the Lyme endemic areas as the Northeast and Mid-Atlantic, North Central States, and the West Coast, but it is important to note that Lyme disease has been reported in almost every state in the country and is prevalent in many countries, especially in many parts of Europe.

Lyme disease is caused by the bite of a deer tick infected by the *Borrelia burgdorferi* spirochete, but there can be other parasites and co-infections present such as *Bartonella, Babesia,* and *Ehrlichia.* Because Lyme antibodies are difficult to detect with traditional blood tests, it can be easily missed and thereby progress to mid or late-stage Lyme disease. It is this presentation of Lyme disease that can result in serious neurologic conditions.

According to the International Lyme and Associated Diseases Society (ILADS), symptoms of late-stage Lyme in adults and children include: cognitive losses (memory challenges, word-finding problems, slow processing of information), seizures, irritability, rage attacks, anxiety, depression, rapid mood swings that mimic bipolar disorder, or behaviors and symptoms that suggest possible AD/HD or autism.

It's important for parents to know that, further complicating this issue, the clinical diagnosis of late-stage Lyme disease and the efficacy of more sophisticated blood tests available are still controversial within some medical circles, as is the standard late-stage neurologic Lyme treatment regimen of long-term antibiotics.

The Sensory Profile: Contributing Characteristics

Now that we have an understanding of some of the common diagnoses, I want to show you the ways many sensory profiles are related. The first step in this process begins with understanding the common factors that are present for many sensory kids.

The Genetic Component. Many of the diagnoses described above (with the exception of Lyme disease and PANDAS) also have a genetic component. This means that your anxiety may be a piece of your Asperger's child's experience, or it may even explain why your typical child, though not living with a diagnosis, may have anxious tendencies. Uncle Bob's AD/HD may give you information about how your child's impulsivity or distractibility may develop and present over the years. Since 1 in 4 Americans live with a mental health issue, there are not many families that do not have someone (or two someones) impacted by one of the neurological disorders that are prevalent in our children today.

Coexisting Conditions. These issues aren't diagnosed in a vacuum. The other common and complicating factor with many of these neurological disorders is the high incidence of a coexisting, or comorbid, condition. The Centers for Disease Control states that as many as 50 percent of kids diagnosed with AD/HD also have a coexisting condition. The National Alliance of Mental Illness (NAMI) lists the most common coexisting conditions as learning disorder, oppositional defiant disorder (ODD), conduct disorders, anxiety disorders, and depression. So many times, parents of sensory kids with one diagnosis, like AD/HD, are also learning how to support additional challenges. This can make supporting your child even more complicated.

Secondary Symptoms. Although some of our sensory kids are living with just one disorder, they often develop secondary symptoms as a result of living with the challenges associated with their primary disorder. For example, a child with AD/HD may learn that sitting for long periods is hard for her and she always seems to get into trouble, so she may develop anxiety about taking part in any activity that involves being still and focusing for long periods of time.

Inconsistency. One of the most consistent pieces about neurological disorders is the inconsistent presentation of symptoms and challenges. This can be one of the hardest things for many people to understand when living with or supporting a sensory child. They can have periods of being connected, attentive, and calm that can trick us into believing that they are "getting better" or outgrowing their challenges. Unfortunately, this is usually not the case, but just an example of the common inconsistencies we will see while parenting our sensory kids. When creating Sensory Organizing systems, we will be working around supporting our sensory children during their most challenging times.

The Sensory Profile: Different Diagnoses, but the Same Core Challenges

Now that we have a basic understanding of some common neurological profiles, I want to highlight the overlapping behavioral challenges we might see when supporting different types of sensory kids at home. What makes it so complicated for parents, teachers, and even clinicians is that many of the behaviors in the diagnoses mentioned above are present in multiple diagnoses. This can make it difficult to understand the subtle differences in behavioral presentations and tough to get a clear sense of primary versus secondary symptoms. The simple fact is that most sensory kids are living with some combination of the behaviors outlined below. This reality becomes the basis for why the Sensory Organizing techniques you will learn about in this book focus on the behavior rather than strictly on the diagnosis. Here, my goal is to show you the common overlapping challenges. As we move into chapter 3, I will show you how to sort through this information to create simple solutions for your child's unique sensory presentation.

Let's take a look at the common core challenges/behaviors and how they might manifest themselves in different diagnostic profiles.

Attentional Challenges. Many sensory kids are living with attentional challenges. This can exist as either a primary symptom of impulsive or distracted behavior (as with an AD/HD diagnosis) or as a secondary symptom (like in children with anxiety disorder where their "worries" can cause them to have difficulty focusing on the task at hand). Depending on a child's primary diagnosis, there could be many different reasons for their seeming inattentive.

- SPD: These kids may seem distracted and/or impulsive as they are navigating sensory information that is overwhelming or confusing to them.
- AD/HD: The hallmark symptoms of AD/HD are impulsive and/or distracted behavior, difficulties staying on task, and having a hard time controlling the "gotta do it's."
- Anxiety disorder: Because kids with anxiety can be internally focused on worries and/or obsessions, they may appear to be distracted or hard to keep on task.
- ASD/Asperger's: They can seem distracted and impulsive because they are internally focused as they navigate a situation or think about one of their special interests.
- Bipolar disorder and other mood disorders: Kids with mood disorders can be so focused on the current mood they are in, either mania phase, depressive phase, or anywhere in between, that they seem distracted or internally focused.

Rigid/Inflexible. *Rigidity* is a word you hear a lot with regard to sensory kids. They often have challenges transitioning into new activities and need things to be a certain way. They don't handle change or spontaneity well, and this leaves many sensory kids rigid in their expectations and inflexible with changes to their internal plans.

- SPD: They can be rigid or inflexible during new situations and transitions when there are intense levels of sensory input.

- AD/HD: Because of their internal need for the new and exciting, AD/HD kids can be inflexible when doing the same old thing. They can also have a hard time getting started on a new task especially when it is something that seems either overwhelming or unexciting.
- Anxiety disorder: These kids can have a strong pull toward what is comfortable, safe, and/or ritualistic. As a result, they can be very rigid and inflexible when it comes to doing something a new way or trying a new experience.
- ASD/Asperger's: The tendencies to have restrictive interests, difficulties dealing with unpredictability, and repetitive thoughts and actions can make transitioning to different activities and situations difficult.
- Bipolar disorder and other mood disorders: Chronic irritability can be a big piece of living with bipolar disorder and other mood disorders, and usually comes out during transitions or when engaging in an undesired activity.

Anxious or Overwhelmed. Worry or internal repetitive thoughts leave many sensory kids feeling overwhelmed or panicked about daily experiences. As mentioned earlier, anxiety can come as a primary diagnosis, but it is also very common as a secondary challenge for many sensory profiles. This can leave many sensory kids constantly feeling like they don't understand or are unprepared for many day-to-day activities.

- SPD: The challenges SPD kids have in processing sensory information can leave them feeling confused, overwhelmed, and anxious in many situations.
- AD/HD: These sensory kids generally do well with the initial excitement of new people and places. They will have challenges when they are in the same situation for long periods. The anxiety can come in when they are expected to know how to complete a task and/or handle a situation they have learned is hard for them. They can be prone to worry—a place where their mind can go when not doing something else.

- Anxiety disorder: When kids are living with anxiety, many simple experiences and situations leave them worried, consumed by panic, or internally playing out the worst-case scenario.
- ASD/Asperger's: Because they are moving through many situations that are confusing to them, especially social ones, they are likely to be anxious or overwhelmed.
- Bipolar disorder and other mood disorders: These kids are living with very unpredictable behavior on a daily basis, leaving them prone to anxiety around knowing how they will behave.

Social and Emotional Challenges. Social and emotional struggles are common to many sensory kids. Emotional regulation challenges can make it hard for them to have expected responses to daily experiences and leave them working very hard to "hold it together." Many sensory kids also have challenges with social rules and understanding social nuances, which impact their ability to relate to those around them in ways that are appropriate.

- SPD: These sensory kids may have a hard time calming down when excited or upset, little things may get a strong reaction, and they may have challenges at times getting along with friends.
- AD/HD: These kids can have challenges with interpersonal skills, including sharing and social reciprocity (the normal back-and-forth exchange). Due to the core inability to control behavior, AD/HD kids can have a hard time keeping their emotions balanced, can be prone to strong reactions, and have a hard time processing information before reacting.
- Anxiety disorder: Due to worry about new situations, excessive time preparing for everyday situations, and/or obsessions or compulsions, anxious kids may have periods of being withdrawn and distracted that can impact their social relationships.
- ASD/Asperger's: They can have social challenges due to impairments in reading nonverbal cues and having restricted interests. They also can have challenges regulating their emotions—their

excitement level might get higher than other kids, and their anger or sadness may be extreme.

- Bipolar disorder and other mood disorders: Kids with BD are moving between stages of feeling "better than" and "worse than," and this can make for confusing peer relationships.

Low Frustration Tolerance and/or Explosiveness. Because our sensory kids are constantly navigating confusing situations, have rigid expectations of how things need to be, and can struggle with everyday tasks, they are prone to high levels of frustration and/or explosive behavior.

- SPD: The constant struggle in performing everyday tasks leaves the SPD child prone to high levels of frustration.
- AD/HD: Due to constant struggles with managing distractibility and impulsive urges (and always being told to pay attention or stop fiddling with your pencil), AD/HD kids have a low threshold for frustration.
- Anxiety disorder: Because anxious kids are working with very specific ideas of how things need to be, they can react with tears and frustration when things are not going the way they anticipated.
- ASD/Asperger's: Due to the constant feeling that they don't fit in or that things don't make sense to them, frustration can be a common side effect for our autism spectrum kids.
- Bipolar disorder and other mood disorders: The main goal of working with BP kids is keeping them in a balanced place. Due to the natural urge to be either "up" or "down," BP kids will show periods of frustration or explosive behavior.

Executive Function Challenges. One of the more common symptoms of many neurological diagnoses is the inherent challenge of planning, sequencing, and organizing in order to get a task done. This can be one of the most challenging pieces for parents, teachers, and for our sensory kids, as executive function skills have a real impact on their ability to function throughout the day.

- SPD: Inherent challenges with sensory input make planning, sequencing, and organizing to accomplish a task difficult for our SPD kids.
- AD/HD: Due to being prone to distractibility and impulsivity, these kids can have a hard time staying focused long enough to plan and organize a task. This disorganization piece can lead to a secondary symptom of anxiety for many AD/HD kids.
- Anxiety disorder: The preoccupation or worry about the event/project can leave the anxious child paralyzed when trying to come up with a plan to get something accomplished.
- ASD/Asperger's: Challenges in flexibility and emotional regulation will make planning, sequencing, and organizing a task difficult for ASD and Asperger's kids.
- Bipolar disorder and other mood disorders: Because BD is also thought to impact the frontal lobe (like many of the other disorders we have talked about), these kids will also exhibit challenges in the organizing, planning, and sequencing needed to complete a task.

I know that understanding the diagnostic piece can be an overwhelming part of the process, but I want you to see the connection between the challenges that exist for many different profiles. By breaking down a diagnosis into the most common challenging behaviors for your sensory child, I will show you how to create a tangible framework for developing a plan.

With this book, I will also give you some simple strategies that support many diagnoses and all of the common sensory challenges and behaviors. We will learn that tapping into organization, structure, routine, and visual aids will help you to successfully support all sensory profiles you might be living with at home. Get ready as we move on to the next step in our Sensory Organizing process—understanding your sensory child's learning style!

Chapter 3

How Does Your Child Learn Best?

The Power of Sensory Parenting, Objective Observation, and Learning Styles

In the last chapter, you learned a bit more about who your sensory child is: the common diagnoses that fall under the sensory label, common factors among sensory kids, and common challenges that many sensory kids face daily. However, these insights can take you only so far. Each child is unique, and each sensory child sees the world in his own special way. You know your child better than anyone else does, and that's why you are the perfect person to work with him to create a personalized Sensory Organizing plan.

In this chapter, you will learn how to observe your sensory child and tap into his or her unique sensory learning styles. These tools will help you learn how to dig a bit deeper and observe closely how your child interacts with and processes the world around him. First, you need to create new ground rules for yourself as a sensory parent, an integral part of shifting into a place of nonjudgment and support for yourself and for your sensory child.

Rules of Parenting a Sensory Child

Formally investigating your beliefs around parenting might be the most important step you can take for yourself. It is necessary to create some new parameters around what it means to be a good parent. It may be time to reevaluate your preconceived notions of traditional parenting, as these may not fit into your experience as the parent of a sensory child. Your job is not to compare yourself to other parents around you but to figure out what works for your own family. Here are a few new parenting rules to help get you started:

1. **Your Child's Disorder Is Not a Reflection on You or Your Parenting.** Looking at things for how they really are and letting go of the why or how it happened can get us to a neutral, open place. You will need to gain a level of confidence that these new parenting rules *are* right for your child. The reality is that parents of typical children or members of your own family will question your approach. They are usually coming from a place of wanting to help, but have no frame of reference or experience with sensory children. Stick to your guns! Only you know what is best for your sensory child and your family.
2. **Let Go of Guilt and Anger.** When you are in a place of blame, guilt, or anger, you are making your sensory child's experience about you, and this takes away your power to advocate for them effectively.
3. **Value the Gift of the Experience.** Get in a habit of sitting down and writing out a gratitude list of all the wonderful things you have learned and experienced as a result of being the parent of a sensory child.
4. **Initially, Parenting a Sensory Child Is a Counterintuitive Process.** What might work when parenting most typical kids usually will not work in the same way for sensory kids. It takes more conscious thought and preparation for daily activities to parent a sensory child. If you can be mindful of this one idea, you will be able to adjust and adapt your plans to the daily situations that might be a challenge.
5. **Celebrate the Strengths.** Have a solid understanding of your sensory child's strengths. Write out a list of all your child's great characteristics. Sensory kids are special and among some of the most

successful adults in the world. You are going to run into many people who won't understand or appreciate what they bring to the table—make sure you do!

6. **Parenting a Sensory Child Is a Marathon, Not a Race.** Parenting is a journey and with a sensory child, the journey tends to have many twists and turns. Focus on the long-term objectives and then create the steps needed to get there.
7. **No Sensory Solution Works Forever.** Frequent amendments will be needed to support your growing and ever-changing sensory child. All kids grow and change, and these changes can be more exaggerated for sensory kids. When you understand how to tap into structure, routines, and visual aids, you will be able to find solutions to the changing landscape you will face over time with your sensory child.
8. **Embrace When You Do It All Wrong!** The bottom line is that you can learn more about how to better support your sensory child when something goes all wrong as opposed to the hundred times you do it right. Embrace the lessons in the "wrong" experiences.
9. **Be Guided by Love and Understanding.** Our sensory kids just want to feel safe, loved, and understood. They are great kids who have a hard time learning the rules of life in the traditional way. They need and want to have times every day when they are in an environment that they understand and that supports their way of seeing the world. You *can* do this for them at home.
10. **Pass It On!** One of the best long-term gifts we can give sensory children is to teach them the tools. If you start sensory organizing at an early age, your sensory child will have years of practice, trial and error, and examples of real success. The goal is for this to be a way of life for them so when they are in high school and feeling overwhelmed, they stop and say, "What's my plan to handle this or get this done?" That is the definition of self-reliance (and successful parenting!).

Having a new understanding of your sensory parenting rules puts you in a great place to observe your child objectively and figure out their core strengths and core challenges. Then you'll take it a step further and look at the Three Main Learning Styles to figure out how your sensory child processes information best (and how you can best support his learning). These two steps will give you all the information you need to create an organizational system that's targeted to his specific needs.

How to Observe Objectively

One of the best skills you can develop to provide long-term support is to become a truly objective observer. This will give you access to some amazing information that can be very important as you identify challenges and create supports for your child.

Of course, you know how to observe your child—you have been watching over his every move for years. But to start the Sensory Organizing process, you need to learn how to observe *objectively*—a slightly different (and very important) skill. Here are a few quick guidelines to keep in mind when observing your child:

Learn to Detach Emotionally. This is a tough one. You need to look at your child with "fresh" eyes. Take a deep breath, open your eyes, and pretend you are watching someone else's child for a moment. You may want to physically step back from the group of parents or kids as they are playing. The goal: you want to detach and become a person observing a person instead of a parent watching a child. This one step will allow you to see things from a place of truth, not a place of feeling, judgment, or emotion.

Observe from a Place of Compassion But Not Empathy. As you're watching your child, try to observe without empathy. This sounds strange at first to parents: isn't it our *job* to be empathetic? Often, yes, but not in this moment. Consider this: When we observe from a place of compassion, we are able to be sympathetic toward someone else's experiences. When we observe from a place of empathy, we are not only feeling sympathetic toward someone else's experience but also trying to share the feeling they are having. However, being too caught up in our sensory child's experience deeply removes our ability to objectively address the challenge that they are having.

Resist the Urge to Jump in and Fix Everything Immediately. Sometimes the best information we get is from an experience that went all wrong. The gift in doing something incorrectly is the clarity you can experience after the fact. This is true for you as a parent and true for your sensory child as she begins to learn from the varied situations and experiences she navigates every day. Resist the urge to jump in and fix a situation or change the direction of an interaction. As long as no one is getting hurt physically or verbally, see how different situations play out. This can help you see the big picture of a challenge and create a more useful support. It also lets us see progress as we allow our children to work through a difficult process successfully by themselves. We have to give them support, but let them learn by doing as well. The ultimate goal is an independent ability to manage challenging situations.

Move into a Place of Understanding and Support. Your goal here is not to fix your sensory child but to understand where they are coming from, the situations where they connect and shine, the consistent challenges they have, and where supports might fit into their experiences. We *can* make things better for our child, our family, and ourselves but we have to embrace and appreciate who our sensory child is here and now. Sensory children have so much to offer, and our job is to help them bring out their best.

Journal to Learn the Triggers and Behavior Patterns

Now that we have discussed how to be an objective observer, you can begin to journal what you observe with your child's behavior. Journaling is a concrete, visual process to record what we are seeing in a matter-of-fact, nonjudgmental way. Doctors and therapists often prescribe journaling as a way to keep track of our own behaviors. Have you ever kept track of your eating for any length of time? Once you start writing down what really goes in your mouth, the results can be surprising; so much of that part of our day is automatic. Once we see the truth (and the patterns) on paper—for instance, that 4:00 p.m. chocolate craving—we can take steps to anticipate and deal with it.

The same is true for being aware of our sensory child's challenges. Journaling his behavior can allow us to see patterns in a way we are not capable of doing with just our thoughts—especially when we are dealing with an aspect of our lives that might be hard to acknowledge or come to terms with.

Getting Started

Journaling can be a big part of confirming sensory needs. It helps you learn the patterns and the triggers for your sensory child's behavior, and helps you develop ways to get the appropriate supports in place. A few guidelines to help you get started:

Type of Journal. There are many choices available—try to be thoughtful about what type of journal would work best for you.

Simple Spiral Notebook: buy a small one to make it easily portable.
Bound Journal: a blank, bound journal would also work.
Weekly Desk Planner: this would give you more structured dates to notate events.
Smartphone Notes: Journal on your smartphone under the notes section or download one of the many journal apps for smart phones.

When to Journal. When to journal really depends on what works best for you and your schedule. Our main goal is to get some regular input, so thinking about the right time to journal is important. A few options work here:

Journal Multiple Times a Day: Journaling "as things happen" can be a good approach for a shorter period of observation.
Journal Daily: pick the same time each day to sit down and write for five minutes.

Journal Around Noteworthy Experiences: Commit to journaling when you have something noteworthy to remember, such as when your child demonstrated a specific strength or a specific challenge.
Journal Weekly: Some people find it easier to do a weekly summary. A little time allows a more objective interpretation of their sensory child's experiences.

How Long to Journal. The last step is to have a goal in mind about how long you would like to journal your sensory child. Again, there is no right way, just a few options that support your goal of observing your sensory child.

One Week: This can come in handy if you are looking to get a snapshot of your child in a few different situations.
One Month: A longer stretch of time will be a better support for seeing patterns of challenging times and experiences. This can also be a help to chart one or two challenging behaviors (for example, journaling around when tantrums happen for your sensory child).
Through a Difficult Situation: If you know of a common difficult situation or major transition for your sensory child, a detailed journaling of such times can give you great information for supporting the next one.

Types of Journaling

Now that we have some ideas of how to get journaling started, I want to highlight some different journaling styles. Recording concrete examples or seeing specific patterns can be particularly helpful to do before or in conjunction with any professional help you have, such as before a pediatrician visit where you hope to get a referral to a specialist, before a developmental or neuropsychological evaluation, or even before a parent-teacher conference at school. (See more on developing your professional support team in chapter 13.) We will look at two main types of journaling styles: observational journaling and calendar journaling.

Observational Journaling. Here you are notating experiences that stand out to you, but you are not necessarily writing at set times every day. You also can write down a quick idea about the system or visual aid you can create to support the challenge.

Examples of questions you might answer via observational journaling include:

1. When and what causes a behavior change? Are there consistent times of day or activities that are hard for your child? Possible triggers could be:
   - Having a new playmate join a group
   - A quick change in activity or transition (Are certain ones worse than others? Why?)
   - Making your child participate in an undesired activity
   - Homework, getting dressed, bedtime, or after-school: Are any of these times of day consistently challenging? Why? Is your child distracted, nervous about the transition, or maybe she doesn't know how to get started?
2. What initiates a tantrum?
   - Is it when you say no or he doesn't get his way?
   - Is it a feeling that your child has that sets her off (feeling different, feeling as if she doesn't fit in, feeling confused about something that happened, or feeling overwhelmed)?
   - Is it when your child is transitioning from one activity to another?
   - Do sensory experiences set your child off: tastes, smells, sounds, or sights?
3. When is your sensory child most engaged and connected?
   - Is it when he is with certain friends? If so, what does that friend help bring out in him and why?
   - Is it when she is engaged in one of her fascinations? Why?
4. What are some of the ways your child self-regulates or calms down when upset?
   - Does she try to leave the room, does she need your help, does she like to climb into a tight, cozy spot? How long does it take her to calm down?

- Does eliminating external stimuli help him calm down? Does he need to go somewhere dark and quiet?

The main goal in observational journaling is to learn how to look below the surface. You want to note the behavior, but also start to make connections about *why* the behavior is present. Does your child always melt down five minutes before you need to be out the door, usually because she can't find some important item (shoes, book bag, homework)? This means that morning is a time of day that will take special preparation and some particular plans and schedules (which we'll talk about later in the book) to make it run smoothly.

The meltdown is a symptom of the frustration, not the cause. If you can get to the "why" of the behavior, you can get to the root cause, thus allowing you to support the deeper issue—not just the symptom. Here's an example of one parent's observational journaling:

April 1: Had small playgroup today and John was hyperfocused on being first in every activity. Had to redirect him many times and help him manage his frustration when other kids had a turn going first.

April 7: John's been having a consistent challenge at bedtime, doesn't want to stop what he is doing especially when playing with his action figures, getting angry and close to a tantrum.

April 15: John's teacher reporting that he's having a hard time staying in his seat during extended work times.

Calendar Journaling. A slightly different kind of journaling is calendar journaling, which can be very helpful in seeing bigger patterns or cycles of behaviors. This journaling looks more like a calendar chart and can be done in a checklist format. For extra information about a pattern, both parents or caregivers can complete a calendar chart and compare notes.

Here are some patterns you might track using calendar journaling:

- Sleep cycles: Is sleeping pattern regular or are there cycles of more/less sleep and/or night waking?
- Overall mood cycles: can chart daily for information on patterns in mood and/or rigid, irritable, or obsessive behavior. Simply charting the number of tantrums in a day can help us to see if our sensory kids are making progress. (Many apps are available for iPhone and Android).
- Monitoring new medications (positive behavior changes and/or side effects), new supplements, or dietary changes.

Calendar journaling can work by using a separate monthly wall calendar, a monthly desk planner, or a calendar app for droid or iPhone. These allow you to track behavior on a monthly scale for longer periods. Focusing on a few behaviors or moods to chart will be the most effective in seeing long-term patterns. This type of journaling needs to be done daily, and creating a code/abbreviation system can work well for notating behaviors. For example:

T = Tantrum
TC = Transition Challenge
D = Distracted
R = Rigid
A = Anxious.

You would also want to notate the days with more emotionally engaged, regulated behaviors. For example:

C = Connected
E = Engaged and Attentive
F = Flexible

Other Ways to Get Information

Observe Your Child in Different Settings. Get in some observation time of your child at school or a playgroup (ideally when your child does not know you are there!) to be a sensory detective. Learn some of the triggers and patterns for your sensory child when they are in a larger social/academic group. You want to get a broad idea of how your child is functioning in all types of situations.

Tap into What Family, Friends, Teachers, Pediatricians, and Other Professionals Are Seeing. Get input from family and friends and get a sense of how their observations match (or challenge) yours. Seeing how your sensory child acts with different people in charge who have different mannerisms and techniques can also be helpful information. You can begin to see the types of personalities your sensory child consistently relates to (and personalities that consistently turn them off).

Teachers, pediatricians, and other professionals can give you objective feedback on what they are seeing. This is helpful because they are not connected to your child emotionally and they see your child in different contexts, which allows them to see growth and challenge areas in different ways than you might be experiencing at home.

Tap into Your Sensory Child's Sense of Self. Many sensory kids are aware from a very young age that something is "different" about them. Your job as their parent is to help them see the strengths in those differences and help them tap into the tools that support the differences. You can also begin to normalize some of the differences, as many times the things your child struggles with are the same things you struggle with on some level. If you are always losing your car keys, it should not come as a surprise that Johnny is always losing his coat. You can normalize this experience by saying something like "The Smith Family tradition lives on—we're great at remembering the big, important things, but have a harder time with the smaller things." You are setting an expectation that remembering little things will be hard for Johnny without judgment and normalizing it by sharing your own struggle.

This feeling of being different can be one of the main cha for sensory kids. While part of the perception is justified, part of it is probably exaggerated. Often, we as parents don't have a clear idea of how our child perceives himself, and understanding their perspective can be a helpful tool as our kids get older.

Here are a few techniques you can tap into to see how your sensory child sees herself.

Create Some Art

Ask your child to draw a self-portrait. Pay attention to the way he draws his senses: what is detailed and what is not. Try to have him do a face-only picture, and then a full body picture, to see if you can get more information. The details might be revealing:

Detailed Eyes (Big, Open, Lots of Color, and Eyelashes). Much research has been done on interpreting children's self portraits. One general theory is that a body part has significance for a child if it is enlarged or more detailed than other body parts, and less significance if it is smaller and less detailed than other body parts. So particularly detailed eyes may indicate a sensory child who is extremely visual. This child may have both sensitivities and strengths in this area: he may learn by seeing, and visual aids like signs and pictures could work very well for this child. Yet he may have visual sensitivity also. For example, a strong emotion on someone's face could shut him/her down.

Detailed Ears. This might suggest an auditory learner—a child who memorizes songs, who can hear sounds very far away, and who can learn and process best by hearing something. On the flipside, this sensory child may be overwhelmed in loud situations and very distracted by background noise.

Detailed Nose. This sensory child may have a strong olfactory sense or strong sense of smell. They may react strongly to and/or be distracted by new smells. This may affect foods they eat, as the sense of smell and taste are closely linked. By the time they get food up to their mouth, they have already processed the smell and if the smell is disagreeable, a successful tasting might not happen. On the other hand, this sensory child may react very well to calming smells that are used in aromatherapy like lavender, chamomile, and jasmine.

Detailed Mouth. A large or detailed mouth on a self-portrait might mean that your child needs strong input when eating and/or has a sensitive sense of taste. They may need strong input in this area to get the appropriate amount of sensory information: chewy foods (gummies, taffy), sour foods (sour apple candy), spicy foods, or crunchy foods (carrots, celery, pretzel rods). Or, they may be picky eaters or prefer very bland foods.

Big Hands, Arms, Feet, or Legs. In a full-body picture, your sensory child may draw parts of their body with very little detail or in a big format compared to the rest of their body. For example, if they have big hands compared to the rest of their body, they may have a hard time with fine motor skills. If they do their whole body much larger as compared to their head, they may have a hard time understanding how their body moves in space (vestibular system) or where the parts of their body are and what they are doing (proprioceptive system).

You can also simply ask your sensory child why they drew something a certain way; it's amazing what they will share with this kind of concrete, direct question.

All About Me Sheet

Have your child fill out an "All About Me" worksheet. We want to get some information about how he sees himself compared to how we might see him. This can give us amazing insight about things kids know and look at realistically and things they are exaggerating. This can include questions such as:

My three favorite things to do/three things I don't like to do
The names of my friends
The people in my family

My favorite foods/least favorite foods
My favorite color
My favorite TV show
My favorite thing to do at school/least favorite thing to do at school
Two things people like about me/two things people don't like about me
Two things I'm really good at/two things I'm not really good at

While your child fills out his, sit down, do one for yourself, and the two of you review them together. We want to show our kids that we have things that are fun for us and things that are hard and unpleasant. This is one way to begin to normalize the self-awareness process. Also, be aware of making this easy on your sensory child. If you know fine motor skills are a challenge, you would ask questions and write or type answers for them, or you could do some of the self-portrait and have them draw the eyes and mouth.

How Does Your Sensory Child Process and Learn?

Now that you have some great information that you received by observing your sensory child, you can move on to the next step of developing a solid understanding of how your child best receives and processes information. This is a very important step in understanding how to best communicate with your child. Is he or she a visual learner, auditory learner, or tactile learner? Alternatively, do you need a multisensory approach that incorporates multiple modalities? Most typical kids are going to have a multisensory learning experience with one dominant style emerging as they grow older. Despite having a dominant style, they are still able to learn effectively using a combination of two or three learning styles together.

But many sensory kids develop a dominant learning style much earlier. More importantly, they are most often *only* able to work with one learning style at a time and can find it distracting or overwhelming to integrate any other input. This can make multisensory learning very difficult for them. For example, when your sensory child picks up a book to read, he may seem 100 percent engaged in that modality, thus shutting down his auditory processing. In other words, his hearing is "off" when you are calling him for dinner, and his tactile processing is also quiet (he's not even bouncing his feet or tapping his hands while reading). This kind of focused attention makes it important for you to learn your child's dominant modality and come up with ways to present information in this way initially. Presenting information to your sensory child in a way that facilitates faster processing will translate into better communication and a happier kid.

There are three main learning styles. Take the Learning Style Survey to determine which one(s) apply to your child.

Learning Style Survey

This test is meant to access your child's general approach to learning. This can give us some clues to their sensory style preference when receiving and processing information, and this information will help us create effective systems, routines, and visual aids to support them.

Most of these tests are geared toward students learning at school, so some of the questions are school based. But you can also use this on younger sensory kids by substituting other tasks that require sustained mental focus. You may be filling this out for younger sensory kids based on how you view their experience. Older sensory kids should be able to fill this out with you.

Place a checkmark in front of every statement that applies to your child.

Section A

______ 1. When I listen, I make pictures, numbers, or words in my head.

______ 2. I learn best with TV or video rather than other media.

______ 3. I use color coding to help me remember where things go at home and school.

______ 4. I need written directions for tasks.

______ 5. I have to look at people to understand what they say.

_______ 6. Charts, diagrams, pictures, and maps help me understand what someone says.

_______ 7. I remember people's faces but not their names.

A: Total YES Answers _____________

Section B

_______ 8. I need to listen to directions for a task.

_______ 9. I like to listen to music when I study or work.

_______ 10. I can understand what people say even when I cannot see them.

_______ 11. I remember people's names but not their faces.

_______ 12. I easily remember jokes that I hear.

_______ 13. I can identify people by their voices (e.g., on the phone).

_______ 14. When I turn on the TV, I listen to the sound more than I watch the screen.

B: Total YES Answers _____________

Section C

_______ 15. I need frequent breaks when having to concentrate for long periods.

_______ 16. Eating a snack helps me when I read or study.

_______ 17. If I have a choice between sitting and standing, I'd rather stand.

_______ 18. I get nervous or fidgety when I sit still too long.

_______ 19. I think better when I move around (e.g., pacing or tapping my feet).

_______ 20. I play with or bite on my pens/pencils during lessons at school.

_______ 21. Manipulating objects helps me to remember what someone says.

_______ 22. I draw lots of pictures (doodles) in my notebook at school.

C: Total YES Answers _____________

Answer Key

Each YES answer is one point. Total your points from each section and write in the section below. Circle the highest number and if some numbers are close, circle both.

Section A __________ Visual
Section B __________ Auditory
Section C __________ Tactile/Kinesthetic

Highest on Visual Style Preference. You rely more on the sense of sight, and you learn best through visual means (books, video, charts, pictures, color coding).

Highest on Auditory Style Preference. You prefer listening and speaking activities (talking things through, audiotapes, role-playing, saying things out loud).

Highest on Tactile/Kinesthetic Style Preference. You benefit from doing projects, working with objects, and moving around (playing games, building models, conducting experiments, moving while doing).

While most kids, especially sensory kids, have one dominant learning modality, it is important to note that if your child is close on two or all three preferences, they might do well when you present information to them using a variety of modalities. In addition, learning style preferences can change as your child gets older, so it could be a worthwhile exercise to review this test at different educational stages.

"The Learning Style Survey: Assessing Your Own Learning Styles" by Andrew D. Cohen, Rebecca L. Oxford, and Julie C. Chi is adapted and used with permission from the Center for Advanced Research on Language Acquisition (CARLA) at the University of Minnesota, and can be found on pages 153–161 in the following publication: Barbara Kappler Mikk, Andrew D. Cohen, and R. Michael Paige with Julie C. Chi, James P. Lassegard, Margaret Maegher, and Susan J. Weaver (2009). *Maximizing Study Abroad: An Instructional Guide to Strategies for Language and Culture Learning and Use.* Minneapolis, MN: University of Minnesota, Center for Advanced Research on Language Acquisition (CARLA). More information about this CARLA publication can be found at www.carla.umn.edu/maxsa/guides.html.

Visual

The visual learner processes best by seeing information and through reading, pictures, and visual supports. The visual learning style is the most common, and many sensory kids will do well with a visual support, even if it is not their dominant learning style.

- For visual learners to be successful at home, take away visual distractions especially in the bedroom to promote a calming environment and at the homework station to promote better focus.
- Visual learners will do best with written directions and/or picture schedules. If you need to give a spoken direction, give one step at a time and provide a visual demonstration of the task.
- At school, visual learners might do well with a color-coded system as well as graphic organizers to help them get a map of the writing assignment or project.
- Whenever possible, write it down, draw a picture, or make a map for the visual sensory learner.

Auditory

The auditory learner processes best by hearing and/or speaking. The auditory learning style is the second most common.

- Auditory learners will be successful when they have a quiet place to work.
- Even though this may be their dominant modality, they may be sensitive to noises and easily distracted by background noises. You can support your Auditory Learner by investing in some earplugs or noise blocking headphones for quiet time or homework time.
- These learners process information better by reading and studying out loud. Whenever you can, encourage spoken answers when giving directions and have them recite back what you have said to reiterate the auditory process. Recording devices can work well for

a checklist of things to do and for taking notes and studying as they get older.

Tactile/Kinesthetic

The tactile or kinesthetic learner processes information most effectively with movement. They are natural explorers and like to figure out how things work by taking things apart and putting them back together again. This is the least common learning style and, since school formats are more geared for the visual and auditory learner, the tactile/kinesthetic learner can have a harder time in school. Some studies suggest that some AD/HD kids are tactile/kinesthetic learners and can do well with movement incorporated into their learning model.

- You can support a kinesthetic learner by using activities that allow for movement while learning: for example, shooting baskets while learning multiplication tables.
- For sensory kinesthetic learners who have a harder time with a multisensory learning approach, you will need to provide the movement before, during an active break, and/or after the learning task to support focused learning.
- These are the kids that may need to do homework or chores *after* running around the neighborhood for an hour or so. They will also do well being allowed to fidget with a handheld sensory toy while sitting for extended periods.
- Colorful checklists: creating brightly colored checklists with an area for checking off completed items is a great tool for the tactile/kinesthetic learner.
- The tactile process of moving chore cards from a "to do" hook to a "done" hook supports this way of learning.

Why Visuals Aids Work for All Sensory Learning Styles

Regardless of their dominant learning style, sensory kids can be helped by having a visual aid on hand. Supplementing their learning style with some sort of visual aid can often help with the core challenges of distraction, planning/sequencing, and emotional regulation.

- For the visual learner: in addition to the visual aid, you can give a visual demonstration of the task at hand.
- For the auditory learner: you can read or have them read the visual aid out loud to support auditory processing.
- For the tactile/kinesthetic learner: you can incorporate a visual aid with a tactile component, such as a checklist to check off, or a tag to move from one column to another when a chore is complete.

Ways to Support Sensory Learning Styles

A few key points to keep in mind as we are talking about what makes sensory learning styles a little different:

- As mentioned earlier, unlike many typical kids, some sensory kids can manage only one learning modality at a time.
- No matter what their dominant style, sensory kids are going to need a visual aid on hand to help with core challenges of distraction, planning and sequencing, and emotional regulation.
- Be aware of distractions with general sensory stimuli. Our sensory kids may get distracted by things that other kids won't see, hear, or touch.
- Initially, present new information to your sensory child in their dominant modality and then bring in the visual support.
- Because they can be so focused on one way of processing, they may need a physical prompt (tap on the arm) when it's time to transition to another modality.

- Often the learning strength can also be their sensitivity. For example, the sensory child who is a visual learner may also be overwhelmed with lots of visual stimuli.
- Some sensory kids can have a hard time with generalization, which is the ability to take information they have learned in one situation and apply it to other similar experiences. This can leave sensory kids feeling as if every situation is new and unknown, even if they have done something or been somewhere similar before. Using consistent strategies to support them through a task or to prepare them for new situations will be a great tool in developing their generalization skills.

Hopefully, we now have created our own new rules of sensory parenting, have confirmed our sensory child's needs, and have discovered their unique sensory learning style. This puts us in a great position to begin to learn the Sensory Organizing process. We are ready to learn concrete ways to tap into our sensory child's inherent strengths while supporting their challenges. This is the roadmap for creating simple sensory solutions that will help you enjoy peaceful days at home!

Chapter 4

Why Sensory Organizing Works

The Sensory Organizing Worksheet and How to Use It

One of the most challenging pieces about parenting a sensory child is the feeling that you are not communicating and connecting with your child at his level. When parents and caregivers are not able to reach a child, they can feel helpless. This leaves everyone feeling misunderstood and frustrated. How can you develop simple ways to communicate and connect with your sensory child? How can you develop simple plans for the daily activities inside and outside of the home that are consistently challenging?

The goal of my book is to help you learn how to communicate with your child on his or her terms, to create a consistent level of connectedness. I want to empower you to learn your child's language and tap into simple, effective solutions that can have a huge impact on the life of your sensory children and your entire family. Empowerment will come from three main tools: organization, structure and routines, and visual aids. The power of these tools allows parents and caregivers to begin to anticipate and develop an action plan for the seemingly simple activities that can create a major challenge for the sensory child.

In this chapter, we will focus on taking control. First, I will define Sensory Organizing and identify the Golden Tool that will help you see why Sensory Organizing works for all types of sensory kids and situations. Then, we will move into a specially designed Sensory Organizing worksheet that will help you see where your sensory child is today, allow you to prioritize the challenges you would like to address, and show you techniques for creating a visual aid or support system that will work in almost any situation.

What Is Sensory Organizing?

In chapter 2, we saw that many sensory kids with different diagnoses can have the same core strengths, and similar behaviors and challenges. In chapter 3, we talked about how identifying your sensory child's learning style can lead to successful communication. Now I want to show you the power of Sensory Organizing and how it will help you communicate, connect with, and support your sensory child.

The Sensory Organizing System focuses on helping you identify the most prevalent challenges or behaviors you are seeing in your child right now, and teaches you how to tap into structure, routines, visual aids, and organizing tools to change behavior and put your child in a position to succeed. This process of tapping into your sensory child's innate strengths and learning styles to create simple, systematic solutions can have a life-changing impact on our distracted, anxious, or rigid kids at home and in their day-to-day activities.

The Golden Tool

As we think about what systems might work to support a specific challenge for our rigid, anxious, or distracted child, there are three main questions that we will always need to ask. This is our Golden Tool.

1. How can I break this down into a more manageable task for my child?
2. How can I eliminate some of the stimuli (external and/or internal) that may be distracting?
3. What visual aid can I create to support the task at hand?

If you understand the power of these three questions—the Golden Tool—you can apply this to almost any situation, physical space, or task that is overwhelming or confusing to you and your sensory child.

Why Sensory Organizing Works

So many "answers" I've seen out there for sensory kids focus on one specific behavior, one situation, or one diagnosis. While this certainly can be very helpful in certain cases, I wanted to understand the big picture—the pieces that made many situations hard for my sensory child and how I could tap into a few main ideas to support all of these challenges. Hands down, the most powerful piece of Sensory Organizing is that it inherently supports all types of sensory kids in many different situations. When you understand the Sensory Organizing process, it really can be applied to almost any behavior, situation, or diagnosis. This means that for those parents supporting that "little bit of everything" profile, supporting two different sensory kids at home, or who have a sensory child with coexisting conditions, these techniques will support all of your sensory needs within and outside your home.

Let's review some of the common sensory behaviors and how they will be supported with our Sensory Organizing systems, routines, and visual aids.

For the sensory kids who have attentional challenges, sensory organizing gives them a clearer view of their day. Regular routines help them learn the process of broad plans and individual tasks, and colorful, interesting visual aids give them a tangible tool to go back to, thus helping them stay focused and on task.

For sensory kids who are rigid and inflexible, Sensory Organizing gives them a plan for the day with the breakdown of desired and undesired activities. Presenting this information in a visual format helps our rigid children work toward the desired activities. Supporting the challenging activities with a plan or routine will help support the inflexible thinking that shows up during times of stress.

For sensory kids who are anxious and/or overwhelmed, Sensory Organizing gives them a "what to expect" tool. This will allow them to wrap their head around anything that might be overwhelming to them before it happens and allow you to help them come up with a plan to support the overwhelming times.

For sensory kids with social/emotional challenges, Sensory Organizing gives them information about when they will need to be socially engaged as well as the times they are able to disconnect and regroup. It also allows you to create visual tools and routines around social experiences that help them learn the social rules and social nuances that are often confusing to them.

For sensory kids who struggle with high levels of frustration/explosiveness, Sensory Organizing gives them a map of how a situation will unfold which is especially helpful in new, confusing, mundane, or undesired experiences.

For sensory kids who struggle with executive function challenges, Sensory Organizing gives them a road map for the planning, sequencing, and time management needed to get a task done. Creating schedules and checklists are a great way to start early executive function training for your sensory child, teaching how to sequence the actions needed to complete a task properly. Since executive function deficit is a common coexisting challenge with many diagnoses, this is a great example of how sensory organizing supports many of the overlapping challenges we see in many sensory kids.

The General Framework

There are some key ideas of why sensory organizing is a great tool for our kids. A basic understanding of these principles and why they work will enable you to create better systems and put your kids in a position to succeed.

Sensory Organizing Shows Sensory Kids You Appreciate "Their Way." The most important reason Sensory Organizing is a great tool is that we are showing our sensory kids that their way is also important. In taking some time to redefine an overwhelming environment or by creating a specific system around a difficult task, we are telling our sensory kids that we appreciate their way of learning. For kids who might be feeling overwhelmed in many environments every day, having these kinds of tools at home will make them feel appreciated, supported, and understood. This simple paradigm shift can be really powerful for our children.

Sensory Organizing Allows Us to Introduce Limited Information. Another reason why organization, schedules, and visual aids work is that they allow you to present only the most relevant information in a way that makes sense to them. By giving your child focused, relevant information—including breaking down more complex ideas into smaller pieces and reducing the number of stimuli they are reacting to—your child will begin to process information more clearly. This makes learning and communication much easier, reducing stress and anxiety for you and your sensory child.

Sensory Organizing Taps into the Power of Pictures and Words. For many sensory kids, the visual learning style is one of the most dominant. By using pictures and/or words to tell the story of the day or explain a situation, you are supporting better processing and faster recall, both of which are helpful as your child moves through the day. You are also making it easier, reducing the energy your child needs to exert understanding directions that come naturally to many children.

Sensory Organizing Shifts the Focus to the Long-term Lessons. Sensory Organizing allows parents and caregivers to focus on the long-term lessons they want their sensory child to learn, instead of getting stuck on the outcome of individual tasks. Teaching sensory kids to use these tools at an early age will allow them to have a solid understanding of what best supports them as they get older. This day-in and day-out executive function training includes how to make a plan and create a visual aid; how to prioritize, sequence, and readjust the plan if needed; and how to build in breaks when doing an unpleasant task. Most importantly, your child will have the knowledge that when they plan and organize with visual aids, they *can* complete any task successfully.

Sensory Organizing Removes the Social and Emotional Challenge (In other words: you nagging!). As we mentioned before, many sensory kids are able to pick up only one learning modality at a time, especially when they are emotional or overwhelmed. Think about what is happening when you are running around the house grabbing your stuff to run out the door, all while yelling instructions to your sensory child and babysitter. Your child is watching you run around, feeling your high energy level, watching your facial expressions, and trying to "see" what you are trying to tell her. She is probably not hearing one word you are saying and will most definitely be clueless as to where you are going and what to do once you walk out the door.

One of the biggest gifts you are giving your sensory child when you create a visual aid is breaking down the input he/she is getting at one time. Sometimes the most overwhelming stimulus to your sensory child is reading your facial expression and trying to interpret the meaning as you are giving verbal directions or correcting them after a situation has occurred. By creating a picture schedule or visual guide for your child, you are letting him take in the information directly without the middleman (you!). This in itself will allow your sensory child to process and understand information more successfully. For older children, this can be as simple as writing a note instead of giving spoken verbal directions or instructions.

Sensory Organizing Offers Indirect Support for Your Typical Children. Lastly, there is indirect support Sensory Organizing offers your other typical, or non-sensory, children. Living with a sensory child can be an overwhelming and unpredictable experience for typical siblings, especially if they are younger than your sensory child. You may find that your typical child will begin to show signs of their own stress from living with a sibling who is easily frustrated, rigid, explosive, or unpredictable. Our typical kids will undoubtedly have many positive experiences and learn important life lessons from their sensory siblings, but we need to be aware of their needs and create routines for them also. By having regular schedules in place, you are providing some normalcy and predictability for your typical child and supporting their desire for structure and routines.

Getting Ready for Sensory Organizing

Living with AD/HD, OCD, SPD, anxiety disorder, bipolar disorder, or autism spectrum disorder really affects day-to-day living for sensory kids. They are working very hard to hold it together outside the home, and they are continuously navigating situations that are overwhelming to them. Because of these daily stresses, they will frequently come home irritable, disconnected, or ready to explode. Giving the sensory child the correct supports in the home will allow them to decompress appropriately and regroup for their time at home and for the next out-of-home experience. This also means that your time with your entire family will be much more peaceful and calm: something that supports everyone!

Things to Keep in Mind

There are a few main ideas to keep in mind as you prepare to create new Sensory Organizing systems for your child.

Look at What Will Help You. Be sure that some of your new Sensory Organizing systems help support your needs/challenges at home. What are the top three challenges affecting you and/or your family's day-to-day experience at home? Can you support any of these challenges with a new sensory organizing system?

Not Too Much at Once. Remember, many sensory children get overwhelmed with change, so be mindful of how many things you address at once. Stay focused on the handful of specific strategies that address your child's biggest challenges. A good plan of attack is to implement one new system every two to three weeks or not introduce anything new until previous strategies have been mastered and worked into the daily routine. This will allow you to achieve the greatest impact without having to disrupt too much at once.

Make Your Child a Partner in the Process. Remember, sensory children can view things very differently than we do, and many of their environments won't be set up with their needs in mind. This makes it extremely important that they have some input in any new system or visual aid we create.

- Ask him what is working and not working for him in the current situation. What does he think are the hardest times of the day?
- Ask him what he thinks will make this process easier for him. These kids are usually very self-aware and can give us good information about what works for them.
- Ask your child how he would organize or systemize your target area. Often your child will be able to give you a clear idea of how he "sees" things, which can help you create a great system.
- Be open to what your child says! Remember, her suggestions might not conform to your notion of what should happen. If it did, you probably wouldn't need this book!

Make It Relevant. Whenever you can, bring in something relevant to your child's day-to-day experience when creating sensory systems and visual aids. Using images of real friends, real places, or real experiences can help them connect with and utilize the new system or visual aid. Our kids need real-world context to help them understand the systems and aids we're developing for them.

Change the Frame of Reference. Imagine if you didn't know any Spanish and were suddenly asked to work in a Spanish-speaking environment without any training or support. People would be giving you instructions and trying to show you what to do, but you wouldn't understand anything. I bet you would quickly get frustrated and anxious. You might even get visibly angry, and your coworkers would likely begin to think you are lazy or even stupid. None of this would be true, of course. You simply don't understand their language. Think about how difficult that experience would be and yet how simple the answer: Spanish lessons.

This is a window into the world many of our sensory children face every day. We don't need to change ourselves or our sensory children, but instead we must provide a new framework and "language" that allows them to understand easily the seemingly "foreign" environment they face every day. It's remarkable what our sensory children can accomplish once we are able to connect to and support their way of communicating. We just need to give them a Sensory Organizing version of Spanish lessons!

Now that we have some context and guidelines, it's time to begin learning the specifics of Sensory Organizing.

The SSK Sensory Organizing® Worksheet

Now, let's start helping you support your sensory child! This is the core of beginning to understand how to change your life at home. For me, and for many of the families I have worked with, the small daily situations cause most of the upheaval in our family experience. This is the piece you can begin to control!

We did some great work in the last chapter learning how to be an effective observer of the sensory child in different situations. Here, we're going to take what we've been observing and put it in a more focused format. This will help you get a more detailed picture of where your sensory child is here and now. I found this to be such a helpful place to start for myself and for my clients that I created the SSK Sensory Organizing Worksheet. Consistently using this worksheet has many benefits:

- By trying to understand and support your sensory child, you will immediately shift out of a place of blame or anger. This one change alone will improve the dynamic of your day-to-day experience with your sensory child.
- This worksheet gives a good snapshot of where your sensory child is today: what's working, what's not working, common triggers, and calming activities. This will help you identify and prioritize your sensory child's current challenges and help you create a game plan.
- By prioritizing needs based on the daily impact, you are putting yourself in a better position to be consistent and stay on task, thus helping your sensory child.
- Since we know that the challenges and needs our sensory kids face can change frequently, this worksheet can be revised every few months to help you improve or change existing systems to support your child's current needs.

Here is a blank version of the SSK Sensory Organizing Worksheet as well as an example of what one might look like when completed.

SSK Sensory Organizing Worksheet

1. What are some of the main challenges your child lives with day-to-day? Are the core issues connected to anxiety, rigidity, and/or attentional issues?

____

____

____

____

2. Do you see any sensory tendencies in your child? Do you notice any challenges or sensitivities around their ability to process information from their senses (movement, sound, touch, smell, taste, seeing)?

____

____

____

____

3. What are your child's strengths, things they are good at and love to do?

4. List the three biggest challenges for your child that impact life at home for him/her and your whole family.

5. How does your child process information/learn best? Visual, auditory or tactile?

6. What are common triggers for your child (things that get him/her upset, anxious, or overwhelmed)?

7. How does your child calm down when upset?

8. Does your child have difficulty with transitions at home? If so, what transitions at home cause the most anxiety or disruption?

9. Does your child have a favorite color, character, or fascination?

____

____

____

____

10. As the parent, what are top three issues you would like to work on with your child that would make the biggest impact on your day-to-day experience at home?

____

____

____

____

Example of a Completed SSK Sensory Organizing Worksheet

SSK Sensory Organizing Worksheet

1. What are some of the main challenges your child lives with day-to-day? Are the core issues connected to anxiety, rigidity, and/or attentional issues?

Seems to have a combination of attentional issues—hard time staying on task—and anxiety around new or unfamiliar situations and people. Can get very angry, or even explosive, when things are not going his way.

2. Do you see any sensory tendencies in your child? Do you notice any challenges or sensitivities around their ability to process information from their senses (movement, sound, touch, smell, taste, seeing)?

Sensitive to loud noises, likes to fidget while sitting, and has a very sensitive sense of smell (which affects how he reacts to food before he even tastes it). Anxiety about trying new things and meeting new people, or going somewhere he's never gone before.

3. What are your child's strengths, things they are good at and love to do?

Loves to read anything, but especially Star Wars. Loves physical activity like jumping on trampoline or swinging, loves building with Legos.

4. List the three biggest challenges for your child that impact life at home for him/her and your whole family.

- Very hard time transitioning to bed at night—can get angry and explosive and doesn't seem motivated by rewards.
- Calming down when upset—once upset, can't find a way to calm him down, trying to talk to him just seems to make it worse.
- Managing anxiety about new things or people.

5. How does your child process information/learn best? Visual, auditory, or tactile?

Visual seems strongest—likes books and pictures. Auditory next—seems to hear things that no one else can hear, but at the same time when he is focused on something or upset, then he doesn't seem to hear anything.

6. What are common triggers for your child (things that get him/her upset, anxious, or overwhelmed)?

Large crowds or loud noises, trying something new, having to do something he doesn't want to do like going to bed or cleaning up playroom.

7. How does your child calm down when upset?

Walks around the house and seems unsure about what to do, sometimes will find a book but does not like to be near people or be talked to when upset—anything we try to do to help just makes it worse.

8. Does your child have difficulty with transitions at home? If so, what transitions at home cause the most anxiety or disruption?

Leaving the house in the morning—gets easily distracted by games and toys in his room when asked to get dressed or come down for breakfast; getting ready and going to bed; and getting ready for something or someone new, the unfamiliar situations.

9. Does your child have a favorite color, character, or fascination?

Blue is favorite color, Darth Vader is favorite character, and loves everything about Legos.

10. As the parent, what are the top three issues you would like to work on with your child that would make the biggest impact on your day-to-day experience at home?

I want to help him calm down when he is upset; I need tools to help him when he is upset/nervous about new situations; would like bedtime to be calmer and not cause a meltdown.

We now have so much great information about where this sensory child is now, what he loves (we will find ways to work these into our plans), consistent challenges (they seems to be clustered around transitions and emotional regulation), and times of day that are usually hard for him (morning, homework, and bedtime—all transitions).

Remember "the Golden Tool" I brought up at the beginning of the chapter?

1. How can I break this down into a more manageable task for my child?
2. How can I eliminate some of the stimuli (external and/or internal) that may be distracting?
3. What visual aid can I create to support the task at hand?

We're going to keep coming back to those questions again and again throughout this book. In the chapters that follow, we'll take your child through all sorts of environments and situations—home, school, traveling, and more—and apply the Golden Tool to every situation. Now that you're an expert in your child's behavior and preferences (how he learns best, how he organizes the world, what helps and hinders his concentration), you'll be able to set up specific supports for all sorts of common situations to help your child perform to the best of his ability.

Take the fictional child represented in this SSK Sensory Organizing Worksheet; we'll call him James. If I were helping this family, I would suggest working on the following challenges in this order:

1. Set up "transition supports" for this child's daily tasks. I'll refer to these techniques as "transition supports," and in the chapters that follow, we'll talk about specific techniques that can help children get through those tough transition times: the morning routine, the homework shuffle, and the bedtime process. Implementing a few supports during these tricky periods will have a huge impact on daily life for everyone.

2. Create an "escape and regulate spot" for their sensory child. This is a great opportunity to create a safe decompression area, or an escape and regulate spot, for times of anger and frustration. As we've talked about, many sensory kids can have trouble with emotional regulation, and according to the worksheet, one of this sensory child's biggest daily challenges is calming down when upset. This is a great example of creating an environment that works to support some of your child's innate challenges. There will be much more coming about using specific spaces to shift challenging behaviors.

3. Develop a visual aid to support new situations and people. For children like this sensory child, a visual frame of reference would be a wonderful tool to help them be prepared for and know what to expect when in new situations and meeting new people. These can be designed for specific situations or in a more general format. Situational aids will help them manage the fear of the unknown, any social challenges that might be at play, and give them a rough idea of how long a new experience might last and how long they might need to pay attention and be engaged—all important pieces of information in the world of a sensory child!

• • •

We're going to keep coming back to this SSK Sensory Organizing Worksheet at different stages throughout this book as we discuss specific sensory-smart solutions and you learn how to apply the SSK Sensory Organizing program to your own family.

The worksheet gives you a concrete way to acknowledge your child's strengths—something that you will want to tap into when designing spaces and creating a playroom environment. It also allows you to identify the top three challenges for your sensory child at home right now. This is where you will get started designing your child's supports! You will gather information about common triggers for your child. You might find these are connected to the top three challenges and that once supports are in place, those triggers lose their power. You will also get a chance to identify your child's favorite things and see opportunities to build these into your room plans and daily routines.

This worksheet is a great tool that can be used anytime to help you get a concrete snapshot of where your child is today. The worksheet is the first step in helping parents break it down, come up with a game plan for their sensory kids, and start to implement sensory systems.

In the next nine chapters, we will walk through your home and daily experiences to show you real, practical ways you can create and utilize these supports to help make life with your sensory child, and your whole family, more peaceful and connected. We'll learn how to provide support during difficult times of the day, prioritizing the challenging situations to work on, and simple ways to bring in "loves" and fascinations.

Keep the SSK Sensory Organizing Worksheet and the Golden Tool handy as we move into chapter 5, "The Fundamentals of Sensory Spaces." Let's get going and create some at-home supports for our sensory kids!

Part 2

Helping Your Sensory Child at Home

Chapter 5

The Fundamentals of Sensory Spaces

How to Design a Room Based on Your Child

As a parent of a sensory child, you can have periods of feeling completely powerless. How can you help your child transition to home smoothly? How can you make your home a safe, nurturing place for your child? How can you build in some calming, independent activities for your sensory child that will give you concrete periods to spend with your other children? The good news is there are tools to help.

As we said in chapter 4, our sensory kids are constantly navigating overwhelming situations. Because of these daily stresses, they will frequently come home irritable, disconnected, or ready to explode. Giving your sensory child the correct supports in the home will allow him to decompress appropriately and regroup for the time at home as well as for the next out-of-home experience. This also means that your time with your entire family will be much more peaceful and calm.

In this chapter we'll take a closer look at some of the fundamentals of Sensory Organizing: concrete things you can do in your home to make the space easier for your child to navigate. First, we'll talk about some basic supports, like utilizing effective labels and tapping into your child's current fascinations. Then we'll revisit the Sensory Organizing Worksheet from chapter 4 and show you how to design a room that plays to your child's strengths and assists him where he needs more help.

The Basics of Sensory Spaces

First, we want to look at some of the ground rules for designing sensory spaces. We want our spaces to:

1. Support common sensory challenges,
2. Define areas and tasks with visual aids,
3. Incorporate an escape and regulate area,
4. Bring in fascinations to your child's space and into Sensory Organizing systems.

Support Common Sensory Challenges

Let's refer back to our SSK Sensory Organizing Worksheet that we filled out for James in chapter 4. One of his three biggest challenges was calming down when upset. This is a common sensory challenge around emotional regulation. Now imagine that Mom created an escape and regulate spot for James that had all the supports in place to help him calm down more effectively. For this sensory child and for this family, this would be a powerful support for their day.

This is an example of how we use space to help our sensory kids. We want to set up certain rooms or parts of rooms in ways that support many of the inherent challenges many sensory kids experience when interacting with their environments. We talked about some of the common sensory challenges in chapter 2, and many of the Sensory Organizing techniques you'll learn here will support all types of rigid, anxious, and distracted kids.

For example, many sensory kids have executive function challenges, which will inhibit their ability to organize, plan, and sequence tasks to complete a project. Since our long-term goal with sensory kids is to teach skills that will serve them throughout their lives, the earlier the better when it comes to teaching the kinds of organization and sequencing skills that don't come naturally.

The first way to support executive function challenges is to create external organization. You want to establish an external or visual plan that many sensory kids are lacking internally. Look at spaces like bedrooms and playrooms as a training ground for teaching your sensory child how to categorize, how to make a plan, and how to get the plan done in a logical order. Having visual labels is a great way to help support these planning and sequencing challenges.

Define Areas and Tasks with Visual Aids

Because many sensory kids are visual learners, incorporating visual cues into their daily routines will help keep them on task. But too much of a good thing can have an adverse reaction with sensory kids, and too much visual stimuli may have a negative impact. Many kids have visual overload in their bedrooms or playrooms, and this excessive visual stimulation can be enough to have a negative impact on certain kids. We can start to create visual organization when we tone down color, declutter, and define the use of the space, zone the room for use, and create effective labels.

Create Harmony with Color. The first way we can tone things down is with color. We need to think of the visual impact of certain colors. Some studies show that colors can influence behavior. Bold, bright colors can be too much for the visually sensitive child. Lighter tones are the best bet for walls. Yellows, tans, and warm cream colors can create a warm and cozy feeling. These are often a good fit for sensory kids who love the feeling of hugs and tighter spaces. Lighter blues and greens can be calming, which could be a good color choice for the child who has anxiety or feels frequently overwhelmed.

To make a color work in a room, all other coordinating items, like the rug, bedspread, and sheets, should be in the same color family. If a bold color is already on the wall and you are not able to repaint, you should try to stick to neutral rugs, bedspreads, and sheets to balance the wall color.

Declutter. Another way to keep the bedroom visually calm is by keeping clutter to a minimum. The first step in clutter control is deciding the function of the bedroom or playroom. Take some time to think carefully about how your child will use the space (not to be confused with how you want them to use it!). Will it be just a sleeping and dressing area, or will there be toy space or play space also? For example, if your child needs constant support with homework, then the homework area might need to be out in the main living space, not in their bedroom. Once you have decided on the use of the room, you will know what items need to stay in the room and what things can be moved to other areas of the home. By keeping the room decluttered, you will be giving your child a good head start in keeping it organized!

One type of clutter that is often overlooked but is equally important is the clutter on bedroom walls. This so-called vertical clutter can be just as overwhelming as too many toys on the floor. I have worked with some sensory kids who will tolerate nothing on their walls due to visual sensitivity. Talk about this with your child to see what he thinks of the pictures on his walls.

Another key clutter principle is keeping like things together in one area of the room. I worked with one family whose daughter was fascinated with dance. She took classes, had dance clothes and costumes all over her room, as well as awards and trophies she had won. Dance was an important activity for this child as well as a great tool for relaxing her, so we focused on creating an area in her room that would be all things related to dance. We had a small dresser into which we put all the dance clothes with a label on each drawer (leotards, tights, hairpieces, shoes, and costumes). The top of the dresser served as the dance trophy and award display area, and a small row of hooks held some of the favorite dance clothes that were worn frequently. A wall mirror and a small table with a CD player and CD case finished off the space. By organizing this major source of clutter, the room was visually much calmer, but we had also tapped into an important fascination for this sensory child and gave her a great focus for chilling out in her room.

Zone the Bedroom. Once you decide how the room will be used and take out anything that does not belong, you can define or zone the different areas in the bedroom. We know that many sensory kids learn visually through pictures and/or patterns. Creating distinct zones in the bedroom and incorporating creative labels for these zones (another way to get your child involved in the process!) is a great tool to support this way of learning and helping your child make sense of his/her environment.

Typical zones may include a sleeping area, reading area, play/toy area, clothes and dressing area, escape/regulate area and, for older kids, a homework area. Something that might be helpful to some sensory kids and support their way of processing information would be to draw a map of the room to hang near the door. A map of the room would split the room into four quadrants with each quadrant showing furniture placement and how each area of the room is used (sleep, play, etc.).

Use Labels. One important way to incorporate a visual guide is by using labels in spaces (as when zoning a room), and on bins, doors, drawers, and baskets, so your child has a simple image to support their way of learning and processing.

There are a few different ways you can label areas, bins, and boxes (please see examples of labels in chapters 6 and 7).

- **Use Your Own Pictures.** With digital cameras and iPhones, it is easy to make your own image library of real items in your sensory child's life. When you make it relevant to something they know and use every day, your visual aids become even more powerful.
- **Picture Card Images.** There are picture card companies that have software that teachers can use to create visual schedules for school. You can purchase this software to create your own picture schedules at home. A few examples are Boardmaker, Do to Learn, and Picture Exchange Communication System (PECS). (See "Products I Love" in the Resources section for more information.)
- **Pictures from Magazines and Products.** You can also use pictures from magazines or the labels and logos from products you use every day. Because many of these marketing images are things kids have seen since they were little, they already associate the label with the item. For example, pictures of Crayola Crayons or Elmer's Glue

could be pasted to the outside of a box containing art supplies, signaling its use to your sensory kid.

- **Homemade Pictures.** Younger kids might enjoy drawing their version of an image to label a bin. When they create it themselves, you can rest assured that it will make complete visual sense to them and thus will support their way of seeing and processing. Remember, it doesn't matter if the label "looks right" to you! It just has to make sense to your child.

Once you have a library of images on hand, they can be used for labels and for booklets you might make, schedules and routines you create for home, and situation cards. (See chapters 8 and 10 for more on these tools.)

Talking with Pictures

As we get into some of the specific systems that work for sensory kids at home, we need to revisit how many sensory kids process information. In her book, *Thinking in Pictures*, Temple Grandin, an adult living with high-functioning autism, talks about why communicating with pictures and images is a core piece to understanding the minds of many people on the spectrum. This is also true for many sensory profiles. When you communicate with pictures and images, you are providing real, concrete information, giving your sensory child an image to hold on to for easy recall the next time he is presented with the same task. You are also removing the part of the process that will overwhelm them: an angry, frustrated parent nagging repeatedly to get something done. Nonverbal, visually based communication is a central strategy for helping sensory children be happy and productive. For more information on Temple Grandin and her many books on autism, please see the Resources section in the back of the book.

Create a Place to Escape and Regulate

Many of our sensory kids are working very hard all day at school to navigate situations that overwhelm them. Nothing can be harder for parents than to watch our sensory kids hit a point of being completely overwhelmed. This can manifest in an explosive tantrum, a crying episode, obsessive behavior, or being completely disconnected from the world around them. Know that this is as hard and scary for our sensory kids as it is for us. They don't like the feeling of being out of control.

Incorporating a chill-out zone for your sensory child at home can be an amazing tool in helping your child calm down, get regulated, and transition from school to home or for any other times they are feeling overwhelmed. This is a place to bring your child and eventually have her learn to go to by herself. This should not be viewed as a time-out or punishment place. Good chill zones are dark and quiet. Areas that work well are the corner of a closet, bottom bunk of bunk bed/loft bed, under a desk or table, and even a cardboard box.

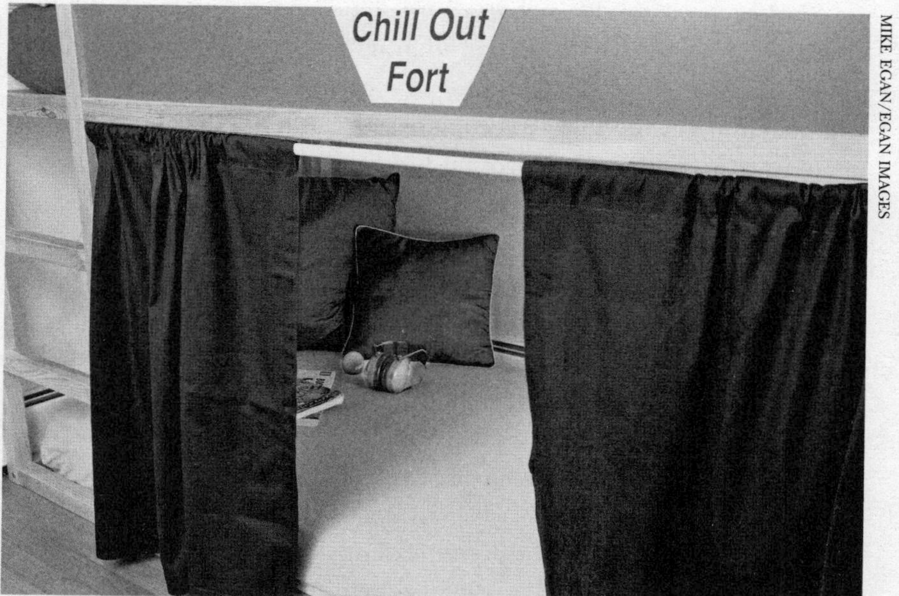

MIKE EGAN/EGAN IMAGES

Escape and Regulate Zone with items that help calm and relax.

Name and label the quiet area with your child and have it contain items that you know are soothing for your sensory child: flashlight with favorite books, noise-blocking headphones, beanbag, handheld sensory toys, and a heavy or weighted blanket. This can also be a great place to bring in a few items that relate to your child's current fascination if you have found this is calming. Remember, this has to be a place the child likes and wants to go to regularly. Having your child help you pick the space and what goes in it will be an important step in the overall success of this space.

Bring in the Fascinations

An important rule for creating effective sensory spaces is taking some time to bring in your sensory child's fascinations. The fascinations can be used in pictures labels, or chill-out zones, but also can create effective organizing systems.

I worked with one sensory boy who had a very specific way of remembering important people in his life. He had a fascination with cars and each person he met was immediately connected with the type of car that they drove. He could identify almost any year, make, and model car out there, and this gave us a great way to create a very specific system that would make complete sense to him. To support his way of connecting to the world around him, we made specific car labels to use for different areas of his room.

Teacher = 2008 Tan Toyota Camry, so his backpack went on a hook with a picture of a Tan Toyota Camry above it.

Soccer Coach = 2010 Black Honda Pilot, so his soccer items went in a bin in the closet with a picture of a Black Honda Pilot on it.

CBT Therapist = 2009 Silver Nissan Maxima, so any current therapy plans were hung up under a picture of a 2009 Silver Nissan Maxima.

This system did two important things for this sensory child: it tapped into the way he was seeing and connecting with people in his life, and it brought in a fascination to his organizing systems. This worked so well that his mom used car images to plan his weekly calendar to give him an idea of what activities were happening each day. Now that is a great Sensory Organizing System!

Transitioning from Pictures to Labels

Although picture images are a powerful tool to use when creating visual aids and supporting schedules and routines, the long-term goal would be to slowly transition from pictures to a written word label. As our sensory kids get older and move into middle school, we want them to be comfortable using more typical cues.

Here is how we might transition from images to written labels using our car fascination example:

1. Set up a system with car images initially.
2. Add written words under each image: "Toyota Camry—School, Honda Pilot—Soccer, and Nissan Maxima—Therapy."
3. Remove the picture prompts so system is working just off the written word/label.

Creating Harmonious Spaces

Assuming that some of your sensory child's challenges involve transitions and tasks at home, a natural place to begin will be the rooms our kids spend the most time in: bedrooms and playrooms. Take a moment to review the Sensory Organizing Worksheet that you filled out in chapter 4. In the next two chapters, we will take this same worksheet and apply it to your sensory child's bedroom and playroom. Here are some of the specific questions from the worksheet you want to look at in detail when planning your child's space, to ensure it meets their specific needs:

Identify Main Triggers

What are the common triggers for your child in their bedroom and play area? What does your child typically find upsetting, frustrating, or overwhelming? Is it getting dressed? Finding toys? Having no place to go when upset? For James, our sensory child from chapter 4, we know that some of his main triggers are large crowds and loud noises, trying something new, or having to do certain undesired activities at home like going to bed and cleaning up the toy room. So for this family, a great place to start would be building in supports around going to bed and cleaning the toy room.

Build in Calming Activities

How does your child calm down when he's upset, and what are the activities he loves to do or things he loves to play with? How can you build these into the bedroom and playroom? James loves *Star Wars*, Legos, and physical activity. That gives us great information about what to bring into his bedroom and playroom spaces. We also know that James does not like to be near people or talked to when he is upset but will sometimes find a book to look at, so having some *Star Wars* books in his escape and regulate spot would be a helpful tool for him.

What Will Help You

What are the top three challenges affecting your sensory child during the day? This is an important one for parents to examine, since it has the potential to produce the biggest immediate impact. For James's parents, the biggest needs are around the transition to bedtime, helping him calm down when upset, and managing anxiety about new people or situations. This is a very manageable place to start and one that will support the whole family.

Not Too Much at Once

At first, stay focused on the handful of specific strategies that address your child's biggest challenges. Zero in on a couple of things that will make your home life calmer and more productive. A good plan of attack is to implement one new system every two to three weeks. This will allow you to achieve the greatest impact without having to do a whole bedroom and playroom overhaul all at once.

Design the Room Based on Your Child, Not on You

Sometimes we have a specific vision of how our child's room should look based on a magazine picture or design show or how our own rooms were when we were children. We need to let that vision go and tap into how our child actually uses the room. Take some time to watch how your child does certain things. Where does she like to get dressed and undressed? Where does she like to play? Does she have a favorite area in the room? (This could be a great spot for the "chill zone.") If your child loves tight spaces, is there a natural nook in the room that would create a "cocoon space" for a bed? Noticing some of these existing tendencies will help with furniture placement and activity setup, allowing the room to work most effectively for your child.

Sometimes the solutions are almost absurdly easy. It just takes your observational skills (remember those from earlier in the book) to connect the dots. I worked with one mother who was having a real problem getting her child to put his clothes in the hamper. We talked about where the child was actually getting undressed, moved the hamper to that area, and the problem was solved!

Make Your Child a Partner in the Process

Remember that our sensory children can view things very differently than we do, and many of their environments won't be set up with their needs in mind. This makes it extremely important that they have a role in designing their bedroom space and systems. One of the worst things you can do to a sensory child is to completely change her room and "surprise" her. Cue the meltdown! Your child should have a role in the changes. Younger kids can help with colors and furniture placement, and older kids can usually give you great information on what is not working with the current room plan.

Ways to Involve Your Child

- Ask him what he likes or doesn't about the bedroom or playroom now.

- Ask what is hard to do in the room now: getting dressed, finding toys, cleaning up, and "chilling out." Focus on those areas first.
- Ask your child how he would organize and categorize items in his room. Often your child will be able to give you a clear idea of how he "sees" things, which can help you create a great system.
- Show your child pictures of furniture you are considering in magazines or online to see what he prefers.
- Look for consistent calming activities, sensory exercises, and fascinations your sensory child loves and think of ways to incorporate them into the bedroom and playroom.

One family I worked with showed me how important this part of the process is to overall success. Mom and I were organizing her son's huge collection of action figures into clear bins. Mom and I were thinking of categorizing by type of action hero; in other words, Rescue Heroes, Superheroes, Transformers, et cetera. When we asked her son how he would like to organize the action figures, he said by eye color: all the green-eyed figures in one bin, red eyes in another, and so on. Mom and I made labels of eyes and colored them in the appropriate color, and a very successful system was born—one we never would have come up with unless we had asked the child.

Focus on the Overall Success and Not the Minor Details

One of the biggest mistakes we can make as parents is having unrealistic expectations of what our sensory kids are capable of managing successfully. The main focus should be on getting the task done with minimal anguish for you and your child all while supporting their inherent challenges and creating great lifelong teaching tools. Having your child get clothes into the correct bins is more important than the clothes being perfectly folded in each bin. Small, simple steps are teaching our sensory kids to be contributing members of the household, develop important self-help skills, and feel good when they successfully complete a task.

Now we understand the basic goals around designing sensory spaces: supporting sensory challenges, incorporating visual aids, creating an escape and regulate area, and helping your sensory child connect to the environment by bringing in his fascinations. These guidelines give us the roadmap to get started as we move on to the detailed strategies for organizing and storage systems for the sensory bedroom space.

Chapter 6

Sensory Organizing and Storage Systems for the Bedroom

Thinking Beyond the Bureau

Now that we have reviewed the fundamentals of creating sensory spaces, we can begin to look at specific sensory systems for the bedroom. Nothing can bring sensory kids and their parents to tears more easily than the ongoing battle to keep the bedroom tidy. Even though sensory kids like spaces that are clean and organized, keeping the bedroom picked up can be frustrating for them. Your child's bedroom can give you a great snapshot of strengths and challenges in day-to-day functioning, and because it's a relatively small and self-contained space, it's the perfect place to begin building in some simple sensory supports.

Before we start, let's review the Golden Tool from chapter 4. We need to keep this in mind when creating any sensory system.

1. How can I break this down into a more manageable task for my child?
2. How can I eliminate some of the stimuli (external and/or internal) that may be distracting?
3. What visual aid can I create to support the task at hand?

We'll look at a few tools that will help you answer each of these questions for your child in his bedroom area: getting the right storage

bins, tapping into creative clothes storage, and bringing in pe
sual aids.

Bins, Boxes, and Baskets

For most sensory kids, big storage baskets, boxes, or bins don't work. Asking them to dig through a huge, visually overwhelming bin, stuffed with all sorts of different toys, to find one specific item (which may or may not be there in the first place) is just asking for a meltdown. Lose the big bins. Your child needs smaller containers that are see-through or that you can label with a picture or a word. Also, each container should hold distinct items (one box for cars; one for action figures, etc.). Don't mix everything together.

I use clear bins whenever possible because they give the child more immediate visual information. There's less to process and navigate. When you add a label to the bin that includes a picture or two, along

MIKE EGAN/EGAN IMAGES

Clear Lego Bin with Descriptive Label.

The Picture Communication Symbols © 1981–2013 by Mayer-Johnson LLC. All Rights Reserved Worldwide. Used with permission. Boardmaker™ is a trademark of Mayer-Johnson LLC.

with a few words that reinforce the purpose of that bin, you take the guesswork out of its use.

For example, one bin might be used just for Legos. It could have a picture of a Lego toy, with the words: "Build : Clean Up : Put Away." This tells your child a few important ideas with just a couple of words. Yes, the Legos go here. But you are also setting the *expectation* of clean up (of course, you will pick up your Legos, and here is where they go) by building it right into the system. By writing out the sequence of events, you are also beginning early executive function training, helping your child break down a more complex task into separate steps (otherwise known as sequencing). It would be hard to do this type of detailed label on every bin, but try to pick a few chores that are hard for your child and provide this extra visual support.

Clothes Storage: Think Beyond the Bureau

Think about mornings your family is rushing to get out of the house, and you are trying to be calm so your sensory child does not feel rushed or pressured. However, the amount of time it takes them to get clothes picked out and on is making everyone tense. Then the yelling starts, tears flow, and the morning starts on the wrong foot. For almost all of the clients I have worked with, clothes storage and maintenance makes the list as one of the most challenging issues for a sensory child at home.

Many times, just the process of picking out clothes leaves our children overwhelmed, distracted, and frustrated. Imagine pulling open a heavy dresser drawer that is packed with shirts, underwear, pajamas, and socks. Since we know that many sensory kids have low frustration tolerance and high distraction level, this will immediately put them on edge. A traditional dresser system used for storing clothes is not going to be the best solution for this child. Tasks like picking out clothes for school or putting away clean laundry will almost automatically be fraught with frustration. Let's talk about a few ways we can create a better system.

This is the perfect challenge to utilize the Golden Tool. We want to break this task down into pieces that are more manageable, eliminate some of the external stimuli (clothes jammed in a drawer) and internal stimuli (frustration about this task: "I can't do this"), and create a visual aid to support the task. One way to develop a better sensory system for storing clothes would be to get a toy storage shelving unit with plastic bins on a sliding system. An example of this type of system is the IKEA Trofast Storage System. It is a flexible modular unit that allows you to combine as many frames and bins as needed to fit your space. Next, you need to:

- Look at your space and the clothes you are working with to come up with the number of frames and bins you would need.
- Designate a plastic bin to hold only one type of clothing (socks, short-sleeve T-shirts, pants, gym shorts, etc.).
- Label each bin with a picture of the item and/or a word listing the item.

You can provide additional support by making a picture and/or word schedule for picking out clothes and/or putting clean laundry away.

So then, the process of getting dressed is clarified into a system that

MIKE EGAN/EGAN IMAGES

Before: Traditional Dresser Drawer.

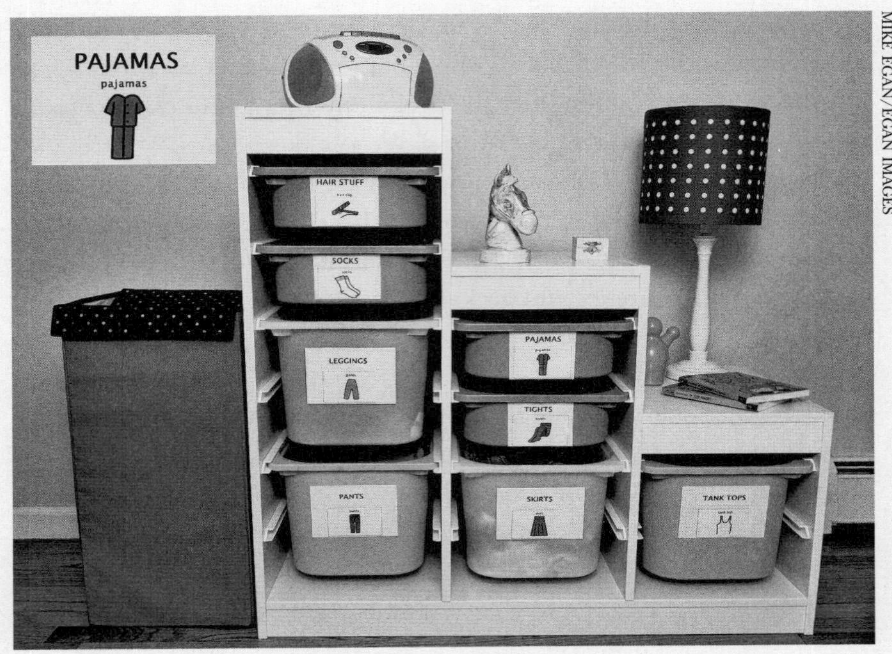

MIKE EGAN/EGAN IMAGES

After: New Clothes Storage System.

The Picture Communication Symbols © 1981–2013 by Mayer-Johnson LLC. All Rights Reserved Worldwide. Used with permission. Boardmaker™ is a trademark of Mayer-Johnson LLC.

your sensory child can understand: get one pair of socks from sock bin, one shirt from the shirt bin, and one pair of pants from the pants bin.

This is also a great way for your child to practice categorizing by putting clothes away into appropriate bins. Again, this is good executive function training. If you can also get into the habit of having your child pick out clothes the night before and put them in a designated dressing area (wherever that may be!), you will have a much smoother process (and a lot less yelling) in the morning!

In the Closet

If space allows, it's often best for sensory kids to have everyday clothes in a storage system outside the closet, in bins. However, if the closet is the only option for clothes storage, there are ways to make a closet function better for your child.

Since many sensory kids have challenges with fine motor skills as well as a low frustration level, expecting them to consistently put clothes on hangers and then find the right clothes each day can be unrealistic. If space is tight, you might consider removing hanging clothes and putting the clothes storage system I've outlined above in the closet itself. Another option would be open shelving with clear, labeled bins. This can work for everyday clothes as well as clothes (or gear) for extracurricular or seasonal activities such as swimming, karate, dance, snow clothes, et cetera. You could also try a vertical six-shelf organizer that attaches to the hanging bar in the closet and provides several cubbies, each of which could hold a different clothing

MIKE EGAN/EGAN IMAGES

Labeled Closet Activity Bins.

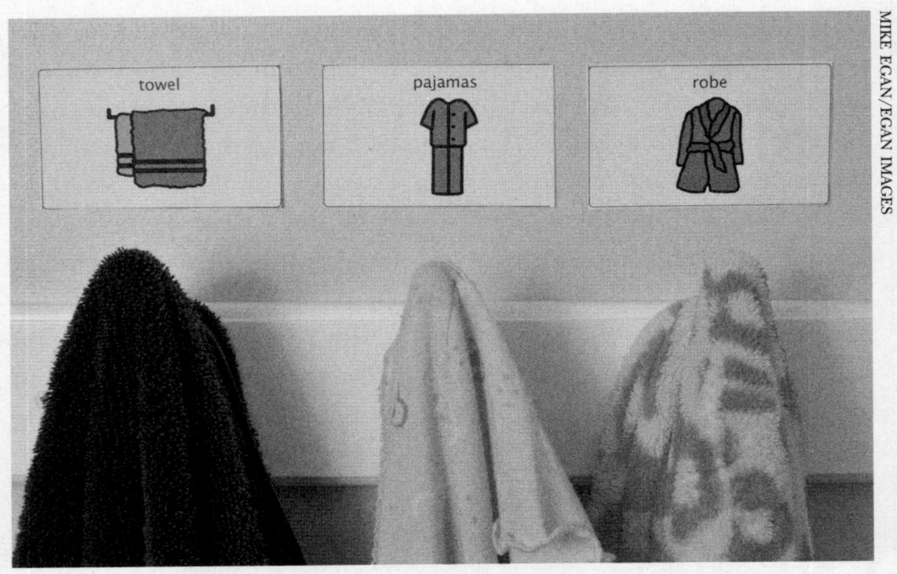

Labeled Row of Hooks for Everyday Items.

The Picture Communication Symbols © 1981–2013 by Mayer-Johnson LLC. All Rights Reserved Worldwide. Used with permission. Boardmaker™ is a trademark of Mayer-Johnson LLC.

item. Again, this allows for visible, open shelving that better supports your child.

If your child has a hard time getting dressed or matching clothes, try to buy clothes in neutral colors (so that many different combinations will go together) and that are easy to get on (because lace-up shoes, pants with zippers, snaps, or buttoning things can often be difficult for sensory children). Take the much more relaxed time on the weekend to practice dressing with buttons and tying shoes.

In addition to the daytime clothes, the closet may be a good place to locate other items your child uses every day. You can hang a small row of hooks on a wall outside of the closet to hold their bathrobe, bath towel, pajamas, or an activity tote. To give your child some extra visual support, you can label each hook with a picture/word.

Be careful not to get too complex with your storage systems. Ideally, if a closet is being used for clothes, it should be mostly or all clothes in there (and not other items). But often space is at a premium, and we can't be too choosy about segregating toys and clothes. If there is extra shelving in the closet, you could designate and label one area in there for toy storage. Just remember to use clear, labeled bins with only one type of toy in each, and check with your child to be sure this isn't too complicated.

The Wall of Success: The Power of Positive Thinking

Some sensory kids also struggle with their feelings and worries, and this can have a real negative impact on their self-confidence. Many sensory kids struggle with feelings of low self-esteem, negative thinking, and anxiety about friendships, their place in the group, and trying new things. Since many sensory kids are visually based, we want to turn the negative "tape" that is playing in their head to a positive "tape." One way we can do this is to create a Wall of Success.

Pick a wall in your child's room and dedicate it to all the things they have done successfully or in which they excel. You can tape off a section of their bedroom wall and throw on a few coats of blackboard or magnetic paint (available in most paint stores) or hang a few cork squares or magnetic tiles so there's a way to affix items to the wall. Or,

MIKE EGAN/EGAN IMAGES

Wall of Success: Constant Reminder of the Positive.

you can simply use tape to hang photos and pictures if that's easier! The goal is to create a space to highlight great things about your child and their accomplishments.

This wall space should be named by your child with a word and/or picture sign. Only one rule applies: this is a space for great, exciting, confidence-building accomplishments. Whenever you can, take pictures of your child being successful in a new activity, hang up good work from school that was challenging for your child, affix a picture of your child in a social setting with friends, or include any images of things they are good at and enjoy doing. This wall will be a wonderful, constant, visual reminder for your sensory child of all the great things in their life.

Sensory Sleeping Spaces

One of the most important ways we can support our sensory child is to help her develop healthy sleeping habits. Nighttime waking can be a consistent challenge for many sensory children. When you take some time to create a calming and cozy space, you can help your sensory child have a more successful transition to bedtime. Here are a few key things you should focus on when developing a sensory sleeping space.

The Right "Tight" Space. Putting the bed under an eave or in a space that feels tucked in and tight can help many sensory kids feel more comfortable. If you do not have natural bed nooks in the bedroom, you can get a canopy or tent top that can hook on the headboard or footboard to create the same cocoon feeling. Bunk beds can be a great option, with the bottom bunk becoming an escape and regulate spot, and the top bunk with a canopy or tent top becoming a sleeping nook.

Settling Down. Invest in some special soft or tactile blankets, weighted blankets, or snug Lycra bed sheets (see the Resources section for additional information). These can help sensory children calm their bodies at bedtime.

Calming Routines. Consistent bedtime routines work wonders. Special nightlights, bedtime books, and sleepy music can help your sensory child fall asleep. This can be one of those situations in which visual clutter can overwhelm kids, so taking some time to put things away (especially toys and books!) can help your sensory child settle down. Having a book bin on wheels that you move into the closet for the night might be one way to remove some external stimuli. For the sensory child who needs a few important things close by, you can get bedside organizers that hang from the mattress (this allows a few things to be near, but not right in bed).

Now your child has a great sensory bedroom! Simple but visual storage bins, step-by-step clothes systems, a confidence-building Wall of Success, and a sensory sleep space will create an organized yet functional space for your sensory child. This space will help your sensory child stay regulated, develop confidence, and begin to build lifelong executive function skills. In the next chapter, we will move on to designing your child's sensory play spaces with the same goals in mind.

Chapter 7

Creating a Fun and Functional Playroom

How to "Zone" Your Child's Spaces

Creating the right playroom is just as important as creating the right bedroom environment for your sensory child. One of the best opportunities we parents have to connect with our sensory child is through play. When our kids are intellectually stimulated and connected, we can have a great occasion to really be with them and have periods of wonderful communication and warmth. A fun, functional playroom can give our children the gift of simple uninterrupted time to play, as well as give us the chance to connect physically and emotionally with our other children.

The playroom is an ideal place to tap into some of that essential clinical support. If your sensory child is working with or has worked with an occupational therapist (OT), you should definitely consult with this person as you are planning the playroom. Again, go back to the Sensory Organizing Worksheet and pick the top three or four ways this room should function to provide the best support for your child.

A reminder on color: Many kids' playroom storage items are bright, bold colors. To keep things visually calm, try to keep furniture pieces light—white or wood colored are good options—and try to keep to a single color family. Instead of picking bright yellow, pink, red, and green bins, pick two of the calmer colors and stick with those as a theme as you set up the play area storage.

Zone the Playroom

Just as you did with the bedroom, create "zones" or separate spaces in the playroom to help your sensory child have a concrete understanding of the space and its function. Zones might include an Active Zone, Quiet Zone, Art Zone, Building Zone, and the Toy Zone. Again, look at your worksheet, figure out how your child uses this space, and design areas based on his needs.

To be consistent, try to zone the storage for each area also. Have a small storage system in each area that contains the items that will be used in that zone. This will give you a great way to simplify cleanup for your sensory child. And since it's often how teachers set up their classrooms, this will prepare and/or reinforce good habits for school, too.

The Active Zone

Many kids will benefit from movement and exercise. It can calm, focus, and center them. If space allows, consider having a place indoors with a few things to help your child move and be active. You may have discussed some of these items with an OT already: things like mini trampolines, weighted balls, beanbag chairs, martial arts "blockers," ball pits, big foam blocks for building and "crashing into," balancing toys, and bowling sets. You can get kids gym rings to hang from a sturdy beam in the ceiling for swinging and hanging from or a small plastic slide with a pile of pillows at the bottom. Some of these items are readily available; others you can find at special sensory stores.

Some sensory kids will love this type of active input, while others will respond well to it only for short periods. Building in these active breaks after school or before an activity that will require focus is a great tool for many kids in managing distractible or anxious behavior. This can also be a good time for parents and kids to connect with "pillow sandwiches," big bear hugs, or building with big foam blocks.

MIKE EGAN/EGAN IMAGES

Active Zone Items for Play Area.

The Picture Communication Symbols © 1981–2013 by Mayer-Johnson LLC. All Rights Reserved Worldwide. Used with permission. Boardmaker™ is a trademark of Mayer-Johnson LLC.

Active Zone Storage. A toy tote with wheels and a cloth handle is a great place to store your Active Zone items. This is easy to label and your sensory child can get some additional active movement just by pulling this loaded cart around the room!

Bringing in the Essential Clinical Support

When planning your playroom space, an occupational therapist (OT) can help with more ideas that are appropriate to support your child and his specific needs. An OT can suggest specific activities for touch, sound, balance, or movement input and advise on the amount of time needed for a successful session, as well as recognize signs that your child is overwhelmed and needs a break from activity.

Label for Active Bin.

The Picture Communication Symbols © 1981–2013 by Mayer-Johnson LLC. All Rights Reserved Worldwide. Used with permission. Boardmaker™ is a trademark of Mayer-Johnson LLC.

The Swing. Some items, like a swing, could be considered both an active and a calming activity (swings can also be a great fit for bedrooms). The beauty of the swing is that it is a fun activity, and many sensory kids will be excited to go on it without realizing that it will be calming to them as well. A swing can be a great tool if your sensory child is overwhelmed or needs a break from homework or anything else.

There are many swing options that can fit in small spaces: doorway swings, hammock chairs, as well as swings that can be put in the corner of a room (see "Products I Love" in the Resources section of this book). Again, labeling the swing area with the expectations built in can define the use for your sensory child.

MIKE EGAN/EGAN IMAGES

IKEA Ekorre Swing.

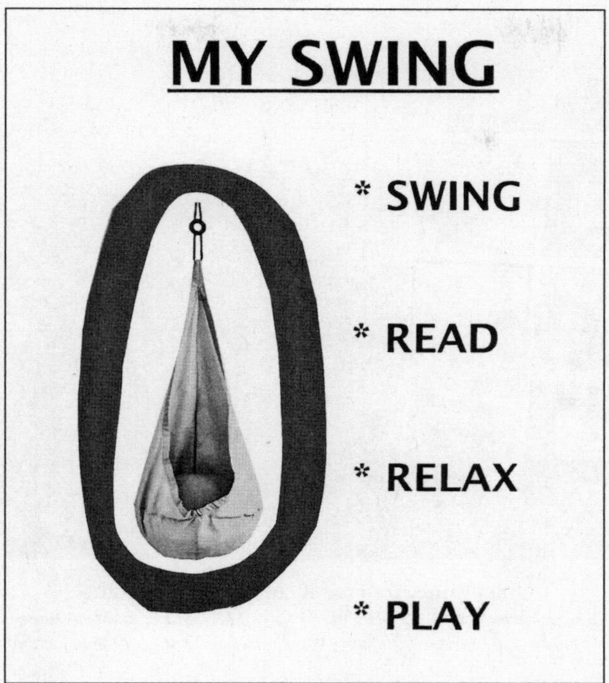

Swing Sign to Define Use.

The Quiet Zone

A quiet zone can be a very important part of a play area. Set up a music or a books-on-CD station. This can help train the auditory system not to be so sensitive. It can also be a great break when your sensory child is overwhelmed and needs to get regulated. A reading/book area is another great fit for a quiet zone. You could include a mix of books that fit into the current fascination. Include a beanbag chair, a favorite blanket, weighted products, and/or noise blocking headphones.

MIKE EGAN/EGAN IMAGES

Quiet Zone Area for Reading and Listening.
The Picture Communication Symbols © 1981–2013 by Mayer-Johnson LLC. All Rights Reserved Worldwide. Used with permission. Boardmaker™ is a trademark of Mayer-Johnson LLC.

Quiet Zone Storage. Here you could have a small bookshelf that would house the CD player, headphones, and music or books on CD in a soft storage case. The bookshelf could also hold the books for the reading area. The beanbag chair or another favorite seat would finish this space off.

The Art/Learning Zone

It is important to encourage and challenge your sensory child's mental flexibility and creative play. A good way to do this is to have art, music, and other creative activities available. Set up a coloring station, and leave it out for most of the day. Encourage your child to alternate between coloring something they want to color (for example, princess characters) and something that will challenge her thinking (a picture of a social situation: say, friends playing together, or a picture of a favorite trip they have been on).

All sorts of arts and crafts would work for this zone: glue, glitter, wooden craft sticks, and paper can be enough to create a masterpiece.

Quiet Zone Label

The Picture Communication Symbols © 1981–2013 by Mayer-Johnson LLC. All Rights Reserved Worldwide. Used with permission. Boardmaker™ is a trademark of Mayer-Johnson LLC.

This zone might be a great place to bring in some tactile supports based on your occupational therapist's input. Try to introduce your child to new tactile inputs to branch out their comfort level: shaving cream, Jell-O, rug remnants (cut into squares for sitting on, putting feet on, rubbing hands on, and so on). Play-Doh is another great material for the Art/Learning Zone. You can also create a rice bin—a bin filled with rice that will give your sensory child tactile (touch) training, as well as fine motor support, when they play with the rice and the other items in the bin. You can include small items for your child to find (maybe little figurines that fit into your child's fascination), as well as small sand toys for scooping and pouring the rice.

Art/Learning Zone Storage. A small table or suitable workspace would be a necessity in this area. If you are working with a small space, you could use a foldable floor table tray or small folding table. Another

MIKE EGAN/EGAN IMAGES

MIKE EGAN/EGAN IMAGES

Art Zone with Labeled Drawer System.

The Picture Communication Symbols © 1981–2013 by Mayer-Johnson LLC. All Rights Reserved Worldwide. Used with permission. Boardmaker™ is a trademark of Mayer-Johnson LLC.

small bookcase would work here with clear, labeled bins that hold the different activities. You could also just stack clear, labeled bins near the table area to make it easy to pull out one activity at a time. For the rice bin, there are many long plastic bins on the market that can be covered (to keep the critters out) and stored easily under a couch or chair in the play area. Also, in order to keep this sensory activity safe and germ-free, be sure to change the rice, beans, or other food filler frequently.

The Building Zone

Since some sensory kids can be rigid thinkers, try to have a zone that encourages free play. Think of ways to support mental flexibility daily. Bring in a building activity they love, but keep the rules loose and flexible. The Building Zone is another place where parents can share time and connect with their sensory child. You can have periods of great communication when your child is engaged in a task they enjoy and, for many kids, building things fits the bill. During these periods of play, they don't even realize they are really "talking" to you, which allows you to get great information about friends, school, and any worries they might have.

I worked with one family whose son loved Lego building kits. Unfortunately, with modern Lego kits, there are specific directions on how to make the Lego item and only one way to get to the end successfully. It was extremely frustrating for this sensory boy to do these kits. A rigid thinker, he had his own internal pressure to do things perfectly every day. He didn't need the added pressure during playtime of having to build something according to precise, complex directions. A better option for this child to encourage creative play (and give him a break on "perfect" thinking) was to buy a generic tub of small building Legos and have him build his own version of the Anakin Starfighter Ship. The kits were saved for brief periods of parent-directed Lego play when they knew they could help their son be successful.

Building Zone Storage. A simple way to support the Building Zone with storage would be to get a small shelving unit with clear bins or a plastic, five drawer unit on wheels. The drawers or bins could be labeled with the different building items: Legos, K'nex, wooden blocks, Lincoln Logs, puzzles, and so on. These could be pulled out of units easily and moved to the building space.

The Free Play/Toy Zone

A very important part of a play area is a free play/toy area so your sensory child can do whatever he wants without your direction. Part of having a playroom for your child is fostering independent play while you or other family members are otherwise engaged. This area could house all of the other toys that your child likes to play with that do not fit into the other zones in the room.

This might be a great area to have a dress-up bin. Dressing up can be a great way to encourage creative play. For the sensory kids who might need a place to start or need some extra structure to understand the activity, you could hang up a few examples of characters they could dress up and situations they could act out.

Toy Zone Storage. A small cubby unit is a good option for the regular toy storage. You could create a picture or label for each storage square in the unit for appropriate items, or have removable bins that make it easy to move toys to the play area, clean up, and move back.

Toy Rotation. For the visually sensitive child or for the child who gets frustrated easily, try to get into the habit of rotating toys in the toy area. The number of toys most kids have is overwhelming, even to most typical kids. By removing some of the external stimuli, you can create an environment where there is less distraction and fewer choices for your child, thus making playtime easier. This promotes better attention to the toys as well as improves play and learning. You can have a few labeled bins in your basement or garage. Occasionally, swap a few toys; your kids will be thrilled to see some "new" toys!

Tap into Current Fascinations. As we know, many sensory kids have distinct fascinations. Others have a few fascinations that change periodically but have a recurring theme. A great way to connect with your sensory child is to bring a current fascination into the playroom. It can be in the form of a book, a poster for the wall, a coloring book, or a music CD. Having these items present will give your child instant comfort and support, and it will give parents the opportunity to learn more about the fascination and connect with their child. Some of the fascinations I have seen with clients include Pokémon, hula hoops, *Star Wars*, weather and thunderstorms, cars, basketball hoops, jump ropes, and yes, safety cones.

One family I worked with had a sensory son who loved safety cones. He loved the color orange and connected to the idea that safety cones created a boundary for him. Safety cones were a recurring fascination for this boy and became part of playing and games in the playroom. Because this sensory child needed lots of active play, the safety cones helped build many obstacle courses in the playroom. They were also used to create boundaries for play and to show the boy what was a "no-no." He understood these cones better than any picture schedule or amount of conversation, so Mom and Dad learned quickly to use them in many different ways to support their son and to create truly fun activities.

The safety cones also became a great way to introduce new activities. When apprehensive about trying soccer, his Dad set up the cones in the front yard and demonstrated dribbling the soccer ball through the cones. That was all it took to get him over the hump. It's not quite as simple as going in the backyard to play catch, but if you are open to your child's interests and get creative, you will discover fun and rewarding playtime activities.

Create Peace and Understanding at Home

Using different zones and sensory organizing tools in the playroom and bedroom will give your child many different supports throughout the day. You will have opportunities to really connect with your sensory child, and have periods of time to spend with your other children, as well as a little time for yourself. Embracing sensory spaces as a place to relax and play, as well as a place to regroup and connect, can give your family a wonderful tool to make your time together at home more peaceful and fun.

Chapter 8

Connect with Your Child

Tapping into the Power of Structure, Routines, and Visual Aids

Now that we have spent some time discussing how to create a harmonious bedroom and playroom, we can turn our focus to the important day-to-day supports your child may need to keep the day running smoothly. Many times, the simple daily experiences are the most challenging for our sensory kids and the most exasperating for parents. How can we incorporate predictability seamlessly into our days? How can we provide tangible, visual supports for the overwhelming and frustrating times? We'll learn how to create a morning schedule checklist to help your sensory child transition into the classroom at school, or how to store all the items needed for a task in an easy to manage package—like a bathroom caddy to help support the morning rush or bedtime battles.

This would be a great time to refer back to the SSK Sensory Organizing Worksheet in chapter 4, where you identified some of the main triggers for your sensory child, as well as times of day that are consistently challenging for them. These are the times we can tap into schedules, routines, and visual aids to create predictability, concrete presentations of information, and tools to support processing and recall.

How Schedules and Routines Support Rigid, Anxious, and Distracted Kids

Consistency = Comfort for the Sensory Child. We know sensory kids are constantly navigating overwhelming or frustrating situations, so having daily and weekly routines can be a source of great comfort to them. Consistent daily routines support all types of sensory kids, as they easily define expectations and ease anxiety. Many parents notice that their sensory children do well with the inherent structure found at school. We want to tap into that same idea when we are looking to support our sensory child at home.

Schedules Take an Abstract Idea and Make It Concrete. We know that many of our sensory kids have challenges with being rigid, anxious, and distracted, and this is especially true when dealing with something abstract or diffuse, like "what we're going to do today." Making sense of the day as a whole can seem like a very abstract idea for many sensory kids. Having similar routines each day for bedtime, getting ready in the morning, and mealtime can help our sensory child understand what is expected in terms that are more concrete. Once our sensory kids understand what is expected and are comfortable with a routine, they will have less to push back against or be anxious about, and they will be more likely to successfully transition to the next activity. For example, an anxious sensory child who knows and is comfortable with their morning routine is more likely to have an easier transition to the school day.

Organizing Feelings

Taking an abstract concept and making it concrete is a key strategy in supporting the way we process and learn information. One common overwhelming abstract concept for many sensory kids is the idea of feelings. Here are a few ways to help your sensory child understand feelings:

Identify

Start by creating a concrete way for your child to identify and label their emotions. Using colors can be a great way to give tangible meaning to feelings. Use index cards and mark each card with a different color to identify a feeling: blue, sad; yellow, happy; red, energetic; black, angry; etc. To keep them together, hole punch the corners of the index cards and get an index card ring to keep them together. Get creative and make it relevant to your sensory child.

Rate

Make an emotional rating scale for your child. It can be a scale of 1 to 10, freezing cold ice to hot lava, a picture of a child crying to a picture of a child laughing—any sort of visual benchmark that helps your child identify where they fall within the spectrum of emotions.

Demonstrate

Talk through the process of your feelings as you are going through them in front of your child. Let her watch and hear you label your emotion (exaggerating facial expressions can be helpful), see how you rate your emotion on a scale, and walk yourself through calming down. Modeling like this is a powerful tool!

A great feeling resource for sensory kids: *The Feelings Book*, by Emily Rubin and Amy Laurent, helps parents and educators work with sensory kids to identify, understand, and regulate their emotions. Available in book or iPhone app format. (See Resources for more information.)

Routines Are Excellent Tools for Early Executive Function Training. Many sensory kids have challenges planning, sequencing, and categorizing in order to get a task done. Having predictable routines and schedules in place will help them understand the order to certain times of the day. Over time, they will begin to learn that there needs to be a plan in place to get many things done, and they will begin to have a solid understanding of how to make their own plans.

Ways to Incorporate Structure and Routines

There are a few key ways to build some structure and routines into your days at home: designate a Central Message Area and work with the Same Time, Same Place rule.

The Central Message Area

If you choose to implement only one new support, it should be the Central Message Area. Every family should have this, typical or sensory! This is the place that family members can access to get information about what is coming in their schedule. A Central Message Area will ground and connect your family to each other, and to what is coming in the day and/or week ahead. Again, this is also the start of some early time management training, something that is a struggle for many sensory kids.

As you are thinking of a space for your Central Message Area, think about the flow of traffic in your house and where your family naturally congregates. You really need to commit to an area that is in the main living space for your family; typically, that is the kitchen area, mudroom, or family room. You'll need to devote a fair amount of wall space to the Central Message Area, and it needs to be easy for everyone in your family to view, from the smallest to the tallest. Take measurements of the space you decide to use, and map out the layout to insure you are meeting all the needs of your family. There are a number of tools you can keep in this central message area.

A Weekly or Daily Whiteboard Calendar. Remember everything you've learned so far about organizing for sensory needs, and think about ways to incorporate pictures as well as words to make this the most effective tool you can. For kids five and younger, the best format is a "yesterday, today, and tomorrow" picture schedule, as this is the time frame they are starting to understand in nursery school and kindergarten. For older kids ages six and up, you can begin to do a weekly schedule to support the traditional Monday through Friday school schedule.

A Detailed School Schedule. If you want to push consistency, get a detailed schedule from school and set up your schedule at home in a similar manner, i.e., color coded, time blocks, etc. This detailed school schedule will help you prepare your sensory child for the next day at school, help them pack what they need, and will allow you include important school items and events on your weekly schedule.

A Chore List with Visual Chore Cards. The Central Message Area can also hold the chore expectations for the week. Having a chore card in this area for each expected chore can be a great support for getting chores done successfully.

A simple way to include chore cards into a Central Message Area is to get two 3M plastic hooks: one labeled "Chores to Do" and the other, "Chores Done." Put a hole punch in the chore card and hang in the

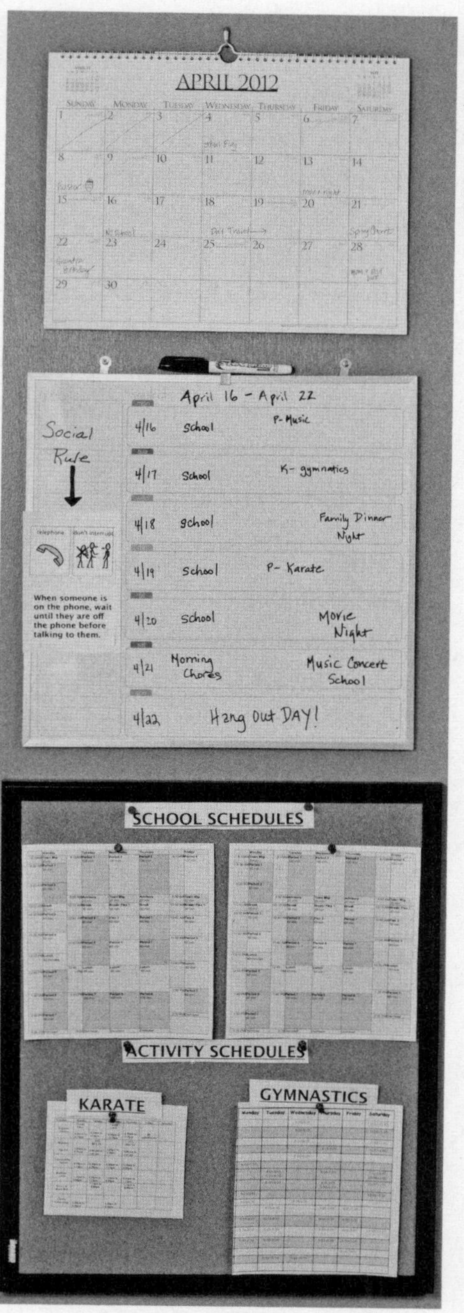

MIKE EGAN/EGAN IMAGES

A Central Message Area.

The Picture Communication Symbols © 1981–2013 by Mayer-Johnson LLC. All Rights Reserved Worldwide. Used with permission. Boardmaker™ is a trademark of Mayer-Johnson LLC.

"Chores to Do" area. You can have a chore area for each child. Pick the two to three chores that each child has to do every day but that are not time sensitive (for example, Put Clothes Away, Feed Pet, Bring Dirty Laundry to Laundry Room). This gives you and your sensory child a quick visual of what chores still need to be done. If your child is doing too much during the week to add in daily chores, you can make Saturday morning Chore Time for the family (remember, we want to set up our sensory kids to be successful).

A Social Expectation/Lesson Area. The Central Message Area can be a great place to incorporate some ongoing social learning as well as the chores, information, and other skills that are taught there. Since social skills can be a challenge for many sensory kids, this can be an easy way to build in some weekly social tips. You can work on a social nuance your child is currently struggling with, you can pick a good manner to highlight, or you can anticipate an upcoming challenging situation (for instance, a birthday party). You can use a few picture schedule images to communicate the lesson more effectively for your sensory child. You could also make a small story using a comic book style with thinking and speaking bubbles.

Here's an example of how I incorporated some social learning into a Central Message Area with one family. Their daughter had a difficult time understanding that she had to wait until her mom and dad got off the phone to talk with them. She was constantly interrupting their phone conversations, then getting frustrated when they didn't immediately listen to her.

Her parents explained to her that she must wait until they are off the phone before she talked to them. "It is very hard to hear you and the person on the phone when you are both talking at the same time," they explained. "If someone holds up their hand to say 'stop' or puts their finger in front of their month to say 'Shhh,' that means you wait until they are off the phone before speaking." To start this learning process, if Mom or Dad was on the phone and their daughter started to interrupt, they would walk over and point to the social lesson for their

When someone is on the phone, wait until they are off the phone before talking to them.

A Social Expectation/Lesson Area.

The Picture Communication Symbols © 1981–2013 by Mayer-Johnson LLC. All Rights Reserved Worldwide. Used with permission. Boardmaker™ is a trademark of Mayer-Johnson LLC.

daughter to review. This repetitive process and visual prompt became a passive, nonargumentative way to respond. It also supported their daughter's need for a visual guide to understanding this social rule.

A Place for After-School Activity Schedules. You can add after-school activity schedules to the Central Message Area. You could also have your child highlight their activities in a way that will make visual sense to them—for example, game days and times with their team color. This will allow them to see the pattern of their team/activity schedule, which will enable them to remember more easily.

A Weekend Area. Many of us are aware that the unstructured time on the weekend is usually more difficult for sensory kids. A weekend section on the Central Message Area might highlight "things our family might do on the weekend" so your sensory child can prepare for what might be coming or can have some choices in the activities over the weekend. As you decide what to do on Saturday or Sunday, write down the "plan for today" on a piece of paper or a whiteboard and review it together.

Same Time, Same Place

Having things in the same place and done around the same time each day will help support a routine and help develop a habit. There are certain consistent areas around our home that can be used to reiterate a routine, streamline a task, and support small transitions for our sensory kids.

Use Timers and Schedules. To set expectations for things like homework, chores, and screen time (TV, game systems, computer, etc.), let the timer be the "bad" guy—not you. It is a visual aid and helps sensory kids understand the concept of time, which is sometimes hard for them. For kids who need a better "visual" of time, you can use a Time Timer, a timer that shows the passage of time by the red "pie piece" getting smaller. (See Resource section.)

> Be wary of screen time and when your sensory child has had too much. For sensory kids, the stimulation of TV and computer, though they often love it, can be overwhelming for their sensitive systems and can be a trigger for moodiness, tantrums, or explosive behavior.

Set Up Specific Areas for Specific Tasks. This can include a place to put clothes out for school, and cubbies for electronics and backpack storage. If your child is doing the same activity most days, you can help him establish a set location to do that activity. For example, clothes can be picked out for school the night before and put in a designated dressing area for the morning, such as on a chair in the bedroom. You can hang a hook in the mudroom or by the door for your child's backpack, so it's there every day when he's off to school. Again, this is consistent with what your child is already doing at school, so you're reinforcing these habits in both places. For older kids who are taking books up to their bedroom, have a backpack hook in the bedroom.

Keep It Together and Make It Portable. Create a portable bin or caddy for things that move between rooms, like hair and bathroom items, and homework stuff. Some examples include:

1. Homework Bin: for younger kids, holds all their homework stuff for a portable homework station.
2. Hair Caddy: for girls, this could hold all their hairbrushes, sprays, elastics, and bows.
3. Bathroom Caddy: a great tool for toiletry management, especially if you have a few people sharing a bathroom who are particular about their stuff! This also allows your sensory child to have everything they need in one place for a particular task—washing face or brushing teeth, for example. For extra support, you could clip a small picture schedule on the caddy or on the bathroom wall for the task.

Visual Aids Support Changes for Routine and Big Transitions

Now that we have learned how to build in schedules and daily routines, we can spend some time talking about proactive ways to prepare sensory kids for the inevitable changes in routine and for bigger transitions. We will talk about how to prepare them for changes in routines, and learn to tap into laminated visual aids, checklists, and booklets to support changes and transitions.

Preparation = Success for Changes in Routine

So what do we do when we encounter the inevitable changes in the routine? The key is to prepare your sensory kids ahead of time whenever possible. Talk about the change in schedule and the new plan for the day, as a matter of course. Don't make it into a bigger deal than it is but do communicate with them and let them know about an upcoming variation to their normal schedule. If appropriate, give a revised visual aid as support. You can also create a symbol or picture for the Central Message Area that means "A Change Is Coming." This will provide an instant visual clue, which will allow your sensory child to begin to adjust to the change. Changes in schedule are a regular part of everyone's week, and the more we can expose our sensory kids to small changes in plan, the more flexibility they will develop as they get older.

Some changes are a regular part of our schedules but still create a major challenge for our sensory kids. Maybe you travel frequently for work, and your absence causes some stress in your child every time. This might be a situation when you create an additional visual guide to support a consistent challenge. You may find by creating a visual map, your child may develop a better understanding over time, and the visual guide can be replaced by just being notated on your weekly calendar.

For example, in the case of the frequent traveler, you could take a simple piece of paper with handmade pictures and words to create a map of Dad's three-day trip.

Dad's Trip Chart

Day 1: Dad takes train to NYC. Picture of train and big, tall building in NYC with a box to check off when Day 1 is complete.

Day 2: Dad in NYC all day. Picture of big, tall building in NYC with a box to check off when Day 2 is complete.

Day 3: Dad in NYC for day and takes train back home in afternoon. Picture of big, tall building in NYC, picture of train back, and picture of home with a box to check off when Day 3 is complete or Dad is home.

You could include a picture of a telephone or cell phone on the nights that Dad will be calling to say hello.

This is a great example of how easily you can create a visual guide with paper and a pencil. You could have your sensory child color in the buildings, the train, and your home. The completed visual guide could be placed in the Central Message Area until the trip is complete. With the advent of handheld PDAs with cameras, it is easy to have a traveling parent send photos of himself or herself on

DAD's TRIP CHART

Monday	Tuesday	Wednesday	Thursday
- Dad is Home & goes to Work. - Dad takes train to New York City - Dad sleeps in Hotel.	DAD in New York City Dad sleeps in Hotel	DAD in New York City Dad sleeps in Hotel	- Dad takes train back home in the afternoon - Dad is home for Dinner!

DAD Will call you Every Night!

MIKE EGAN/EGAN IMAGES

the trip. This can be very reassuring for sensory kids because you are giving them real, relevant information that can help them visualize where the traveling parent is and what they are doing.

Laminated Visual Aids, Checklists, and Booklets

Laminated visual aids, checklists, and booklets can all be a great support for changes in routine and for big transitions that are coming such as a new morning routine for a new grade at school, a new house, or a new school. These visual guides are an instrumental part of supporting sensory kids at home and outside of the home.

Laminated Visual Aids and Whiteboards. Whiteboards can be used either as a standalone item, or they can be a part of your Central Message Area. These are great tools for a daily schedule or for a checklist of things that need to be done, like chores or homework. Items can be checked off as they are completed for more executive function training. Laminated schedules or checklists can also be an inexpensive way to give your child a visual support for a specific daily routine that is challenging or hard for your child to remember.

For example, if your sensory child has a new morning routine at school that is hard to remember, create a laminated checklist. You can highlight the common distractions and give them information about when some of their favorite activities can be done, just not first thing in the morning. You can use the transition time of driving to school to let your child review the new routine and/or they can bring it in to school and leave it in their cubby to help them learn the new routine.

A Great Start to the Day: Katie's Morning Checklist for Third Grade

- ❑ Turn in your homework.
- ❑ Greet Mrs. Smith.
- ❑ Flip your attendance card to "in."
- ❑ Read schedule for the day.
- ❑ Read the "Morning Message."
- ❑ Get your core book (red).
- ❑ Copy message into your core book and write your answer.

Remember:

1. Friends are great, but morning time is not for play. Your first recess will be coming soon!
2. In addition, reading books is a perfect thing to do during "Quiet Time," but not first thing in the morning.

Checklists. Checklists can be another helpful tool to support a challenging task or to assist during a time of day when your sensory child is not at their best. One example of this might be the morning or bedtime routine. Pocket charts can be a fun way to make a checklist for your child. These are big, colorful charts that have clear, open pockets where you can place information in sequential order (please see Resource Section for information on pocket charts).

I worked with one client whose little girl had a hard time staying on task during her morning and bedtime routines. Mom took my advice and put a pocket chart in her daughter's bedroom. Mom created a checklist of sorts by having the steps of the morning routine on the front side of the four cardboard inserts and the steps of the bedtime routine on the backside of the same cardboard inserts. As her daughter completed a step in her morning routine, she would flip over the card (another way of checking off a list!). Once the morning routine was complete, the bedtime routine was in place and ready to go!

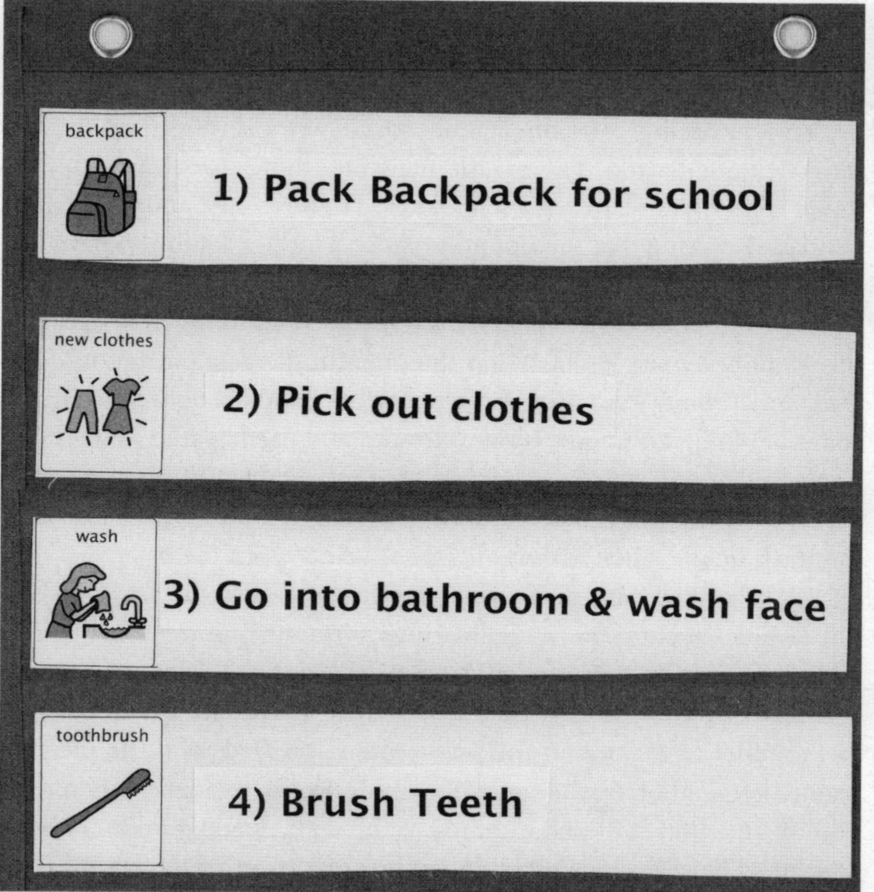

MIKE EGAN/EGAN IMAGES

The Picture Communication Symbols © 1981–2013 by Mayer-Johnson LLC. All Rights Reserved Worldwide. Used with permission. Boardmaker™ is a trademark of Mayer-Johnson LLC.

Checklists can also be used during fun times as a teaching tool: they are useful for sequencing, planning, and coming up with what your sensory child might need when going somewhere. Take time to create a few packing lists that can be printed out and used when packing for the beach, a trip out to dinner, or a vacation (see chapter 11 for an example of a packing list for a trip).

Booklets. Creating a homemade picture book for a big, new experience or transition can be very helpful for many sensory kids. This gives them something tangible to look at with you and during their own time. These booklets can also be laid out in a sequential format with personal, relevant information that pertains to your sensory child and their new experience.

I was working with one family whose sensory boy, Tommy, was starting kindergarten. This meant many new things for Tommy: a new, much bigger school, riding a school bus, a new teacher, and new kids in his class. Knowing that this was going to be a lot for Tommy to navigate, we decided to make a book for him titled "My New School." We wanted to make the booklet as relatable as possible so we used "real life" pictures whenever we could. When the open house came around, Mom, Dad, and Tommy went over to the new school and brought their digital camera. While Mom took Tommy around and participated in the open house activities, Dad took pictures. He took pictures of the outside of the school, the playground, the school bus, Tommy's new classroom, Tommy's new teacher, and so on.

We also built one of Tommy's fascinations into the book to give him a great mental hook. At this time, one of Tommy's fascinations included flushing toilets—and lo and behold, his new classroom had its own bathroom. Dad got a great picture of Tommy standing next to the toilet to include in the book. Mom and Dad used the pictures from their school visit along with simple words to make a book for Tommy that they reviewed with him in the weeks leading up to the start of school. This was a tremendous aid in supporting Tommy in his transition to his new school, and he already had a map of the things and people he would be encountering in his day.

Social Stories

Social Stories are a great tool for supporting sensory kids for all sorts of situations. Carol Gray developed Social Stories and Comic Strip Conversations strategies to support all types of children and adults on the spectrum. Social Stories and Comic Strip Conversations allow us to provide information to our sensory kids in a literal and visual format. We can share information about what to expect in a new situation, what social or behavior responses might occur in different situations, as well as the sequence in which an experience might unfold. Being able to share this information will help our sensory kids feel less anxious and more prepared for situations they encounter in day-to-day life.

To learn how to make a Social Story or Comic Strip Conversation, go to Carol Gray's website: the Gray Center for Social Understanding (www.thegraycenter.org). Her website provides tools for learning how to write your own social stories as well as a number of excellent books and resources on Social Stories.

The "I Can Do It" Book. The "I Can Do It" Book can be a great tool for sensory kids or their siblings. This tool is helpful for all sensory kids, but it's especially helpful for kids who are anxious about trying new things or who need reassurance when embarking on a new experience.

Create an "I Can Do It" Book that will highlight all the successes your child has had in the past. You can get a simple binder and buy clear, plastic insert sheets (for awards, certificates, school projects, etc.) and clear insert sheets that hold 4" x 6" pictures. This will allow you to have a place to put all of your child's paper awards, certificates, and pictures from sports, activities, outings, times with friends, and trips. When your child is feeling down or feeling anxious about a new activity, they can pull out their "I Can Do It" Book to give a quick visual trigger of memories for all the past successes and fun they have had doing new things!

How to Challenge Routines and Teach Flexibility

We know that routines and schedules are important for helping sensory kids navigate their days successfully. But we can run the risk of making our sensory kids *too* dependent on schedules or completely incapable of dealing with inevitable changes in schedule without building in some training for that also. So let's come up with a few ways to build in regular changes to routine to encourage flexibility.

Fun Ways to Change the Routines

Start with the Fun! One night, without preparation, tell everyone you are going to hop right in the car and go get ice cream before dinner. Don't let anyone get anything, the rule is you just have to drop and go. This can be something you do once a month without warning. It's a great way to encourage the positive aspect of an unexpected change in routine.

Have a Flip-Flop Day! Have dinner for breakfast and breakfast for dinner. Again, this can be a fun way to challenge the rigid or inflexible thinking that some of our sensory kids experience.

Have a "Camp Out" in the Living Room Night! Anything that will challenge in a fun way the usual routine will work.

Surprise Them with a Slightly Bigger Reward or More Time for a Favorite Activity. For example, you might allow computer game time earlier than usual and/or let them stay on longer than usual.

How to Build Flexibility One Small Step at a Time

A few simple ways to develop flexibility:

Create a "Choices When There Is a Change" Jar. Say a play date cancels at the last minute and your sensory child is very upset. Pull out the "Choices When There Is a Change" Jar and have your child pick out a new choice for the day: bowling, favorite bookstore visit, favorite park, bake something with Mom. If your child does better with a choice, have them pick two or three options from the jar and let them pick their favorite activity.

Have a reward system in place for times when your sensory child is being uncharacteristically flexible. Say your child always likes to go first and has an extremely hard time giving siblings or friends the chance to go first. Have a random reward system in place for when you see your sensory child letting someone else go first.

Train for Surprises! Surprises can be very hard for many sensory kids. One way to train for surprises is to have them pick two of their favorite activities (you must be confident that they will be happy with either choice!). Put your kid in the car and tell him that you will be going to one of the activities, but that you are not going to say which one until you get there; it is going to be a special surprise. You can give clues along the way and/or point out landmarks to see if your child can figure out the surprise.

Sensory kids are bright, creative, and energetic. When given the right structure and support, they are extremely capable of being successful in their day-to-day experience. Schedules, routines, and visual aids support our sensory children with the right tools to manage their days and get through changes and bigger transitions successfully all while teaching them those important executive function skills. Building in early training for planning, sequencing, and organization will give our sensory kids the essential building blocks to develop skills that are imperative for their success in school and life as they get older.

One of the best gifts you can give your child at an early age is the knowledge that everyone has a different way of learning and being successful, and this is the way that works for her. How great that you have already figured out what works for you! Self-awareness is a powerful tool and can help empower our kids to begin to tap into these techniques for themselves as a natural expression of who they are and how they do things.

Chapter 9

Making Trouble Times Easy

Supports for Dreaded Tasks and Unstructured Time

Now that we have an understanding of schedules and routines, we can talk about using these same techniques to support sensory kids during the dreaded daily tasks and the periods of unstructured time that occur throughout the year.

First, we will talk about universal tools to helping our sensory child get started on a dreaded or overwhelming task. These are also powerful in supporting our sensory kids during the times they might be on the verge of demonstrating distracted, anxious, explosive, or rigid behavior. These magical tools include the Power of Choice, the Art of Distraction, and the Gift of the Fascination.

Getting Over the Hump

Even with training and practice, some sensory kids will always have a hard time with changes in schedule or routines or getting started on an undesired task. The rule of thumb when starting to work with rigid, anxious, or distracted kids is to give them some choices in the process and to distract them from the negativity they have for the upcoming task or experience. These two things can lessen the anxiety they might feel about the change in their normal schedule or an undesired task.

The Power of Choice

When most sensory kids experience anxiety over a change in schedule, they are feeling out of control and unsettled with the changes going on around them. When you give kids a choice within the new routine/schedule or with how you start an undesired task, you are giving them some control back, which will lessen the overall anxiety or be enough to get them started on the task.

For example, your child might have a hard time taking a shower or bath. But of course, a bath is on occasion a necessity! So what are a few choices you can employ to get your child over the hump and into the shower?

- You could give her the choice of a bath or a shower.
- You could give her a choice of the bathroom to use.
- You could have two different bath mats that she can choose from (maybe have one that is her favorite color).
- You can let her choose which shampoo to use.

If your child is in a more flexible place, you may only need to give one choice before she is over the hump. If she is in an inflexible place, you may need to use all four choices before she is able to get started on the task.

Choosing to Compromise

Learn more about using the power of choice with inflexible kids by reading *The Explosive Child,* by Ross Greene. This book gives wonderful tools to parents who are learning how to support sensory kids who lack flexibility, have a low level of frustration, and have limited problem-solving skills—all which bring them to a place of anger and explosiveness. Dr. Greene's techniques teach parents how to negotiate and compromise with their sensory kids and help prevent outbursts and tantrums.

The Art of Distraction

Another strategy to use when trying to support your sensory child with a change in schedule or an undesired task is the art of distraction. This can work well for many different types of sensory kids. If your child is anxious and/or rigid, a brief distraction can get them unstuck from the negative and onto a possible positive. If your child has more of an AD/HD profile, you are giving them a distraction that they may have been seeking out for themselves anyway.

Let's go back to the example of the sensory child who dreads the bath or shower experience. What are a few ways to tap into the power of distraction to support this challenging time?

- Get a shower radio and let your sensory child listen to music while bathing. The focus is on the music, not on the task.
- Make a small laminated picture schedule for the three-step process of showering: get hair and body wet, wash hair with shampoo and rinse, wash face and body with soap and rinse. Again, the child may focus on getting through the checklist, not on the task.
- Get bath crayons that they can use to color on the tub or shower wall. Again, you're shifting the focus from a dreaded task to creating something fun.
- Try the reward of a favorite activity upon the completion of a bath or shower. Sometimes the idea of a reward is enough to motivate sensory kids and get them through a task.

The Gift of the Fascination

As we've discussed, many of our sensory kids are blessed with specific fascinations. These fascinations can remain the same over the course of many years, or they may change periodically or cyclically. I say "blessed" because these fascinations give us an amazing opportunity to not only connect with our sensory kids in a real, tangible way that makes sense to them, but they also give us a fantastic tool to communicate and support them during challenging times. You never know when you will have an opportunity to engage a fascination to help your sensory child accomplish something!

I was doing a presentation when a mother asked me about a potty training issue she was having with her little boy with autism. He had learned how to use the potty but was always choosing to sit when using the bathroom no matter what the business called for. This frequently left the bathroom a little messy and Mom frustrated. (It's the little things that make our days overwhelming!)

I asked Mom what one of her son's fascinations was and she said SpongeBob. I told her to get two 3M plastic hooks to hang in the bathroom: one to be placed on the wall opposite the toilet, and one to be placed on the wall behind the toilet. I told her to find the coolest SpongeBob picture, laminate it, and punch a hole in the top. As her son was walking to the bathroom, she would ask him if number 1 or number 2. Mom would hang the SpongeBob picture on the wall behind the toilet for number 1 visits and on the wall opposite the toilet for number 2 visits. By tapping into her son's fascination, we could teach him how to stand for number 1 and sit for number 2, thus teaching him an important little-boy life lesson and making Mom's day a little easier. The power of the fascination!

Using All Three Techniques Together

Another common time that parents say is hard for their sensory children is mealtime. So let's see how we can use all three techniques here to support a successful mealtime experience for all types of sensory kids.

Power of Choice. Instead of doing a long family meal every night, you might start planning your weekly calendar by giving your sensory child the choice of what two nights during the week you will have your family dinners. If there is some resistance that night, you might give them a choice of where they sit or what music you all listen to while you eat.

The Art of Distraction. If your sensory child has a hard time sitting still, get him a disk seat to sit on at mealtime. A disk seat is an air-filled exercise disk that can be used as a seat cushion and when filled with just enough air, the cushion wiggles. This allows our kids to move without moving. Conversation games during dinner can also be a wonderful distraction for sensory kids. You are distracting them in two ways: first, from the fact that they are sitting for an extended period of time, and, second, that they are having conversations and sharing information with family members. Two conversation games that I love are "Dinner Games" and "Family Talk." (See "Products I Love" for more.)

The Gift of the Fascination. Let's go back to our sensory boy who loved SpongeBob. We could try to incorporate SpongeBob into the meal experience as well. Maybe a SpongeBob cup or placemat would help. These could only be used at family meals, heightening their "special" quality. Or maybe you could make some SpongeBob flashcards that have questions and answers about all things related to SpongeBob. When you see your sensory child losing focus or patience, you pull out a SpongeBob question to try to reengage and connect them to the family dinner.

Trouble Ahead: Strategies to Support the Tough Times

We know that schedules and routines can help our sensory kids navigate their days successfully. This is especially true during the "trouble times" of day. Some of the common trouble times include the morning rush, after-school transition, homework time, chore time, and the bedtime routine. Repeating the same order of activities with a visual support to review with your child can be life changing during some of these common challenging times.

Again, in order not to overwhelm you or your child, to begin with, pick the top two challenging trouble times during the day and provide the visual aids and extra support for those two times. Too many schedules may overwhelm your child and will be a lot for a parent or caregiver to manage. If you find the schedules are working well to support your sensory child, you can always add a new schedule support every three weeks, being mindful of the signs that your child has hit his limit. You may also find that there is a cyclical nature to the trouble times and that your sensory child may have certain days, months, or seasons of the year when they rely on the schedules more than others.

The Morning Rush

One of the most common trouble times for many sensory kids is the morning rush. Many sensory kids are overwhelmed and easily frustrated when there is a time-pressure element, so right off the bat, the morning rush will put many sensory kids on edge. In addition, if your child is on any sort of daily medication that takes time to enter the system or that wears off over time, the early-morning period may be when a child is functioning without medicinal support and is more susceptible to frustration, distraction, hyperfocus, and rigidity. Here's where structure and routine can come to the rescue.

The first place to start is to have as much done the night before to help you get ahead of the morning rush. Clothes picked out, lunches made, showers or baths done, and backpacks by the back door are all simple things to have prepared ahead of time.

Next, we are going to refer back to the Golden Tool: 1) break it down, 2) eliminate external and internal stimuli, and 3) create a visual aid for support. We need to look at the ways we can incorporate this into the morning rush. Since we simplified our schedule by doing some things the night before, let's break it down and simplify the morning rush into three steps: get dressed, eat breakfast, and brush teeth. If you have a sensory child set on eating breakfast first, steps one and two can be switched as long as you are flexible where the getting dressed takes place. We want to eliminate the number of times our sensory child is walking around the house, going to their bedroom for something, or leaving the room to find their toothbrush. These are detours that can complicate, add distractions, and frustrate our morning process. Always think of the natural flow of your house, the common distractions for your sensory child, and which rooms you can use downstairs (if you live in a multistory house) or near the main living area to support the morning routine.

I worked with one sensory boy, John, who had a very hard time getting out the door in the morning. He had attentional challenges and was working without his usual medicinal support first thing in the morning, making the morning rush even more challenging. Mom had two other children to get out the door, and they were on a tight schedule. The rushed mornings and the distractibility issues left John in tears and in meltdown mode many mornings. This was a tough way for this family to start their day. Here is the system we created to support John during the morning rush.

1. **Break It Down.** Create a laminated checklist of the morning schedule and put in the kitchen area for John to review each morning as he was eating his breakfast. (Eat breakfast: 20 minutes; wash face and brush teeth: 5 minutes; get dressed: 5 minutes; shoes on: 5 minutes.)
2. **Reduce Distracting External Stimuli.** The new command central for John in the morning is the breakfast area and the downstairs bathroom. To prevent the distraction and hyperfocus that occurs when John makes trips upstairs, his new dressing and teeth brushing area during the week is the first-floor bathroom. This means John is only navigating two rooms that are right next to each other and is not going back upstairs. Mom and John picked out clothes for the whole school week on Sunday night and put them in a labeled plastic bin/drawer system in the first-floor bathroom. To complete the dressing process and push consistency, Mom put a small clothes hamper for pajamas in the bathroom. Mom also bought John a second toothbrush and toothpaste to keep in the downstairs bathroom. Since John likes to have breakfast first and slowly wake up while eating and sitting at the table, we built in the longest chunk of time for this part of the process (20 minutes). When he is done eating, John goes to the first-floor bathroom to get dressed and brush teeth.
3. **Create a Visual Aid for the Task at Hand.** We have created a few visuals to support John's new streamlined morning routine. We created the laminated sequential word schedule that hangs on the bathroom wall:

Morning Routine

1) Wash face, brush teeth, and brush hair

2) PJ's off and into hamper

3) Clothes out from drawer of the day and get dressed

We also have a visual support with the labeled plastic drawer unit. The drawers are labeled Monday through Friday, which eliminates another decision that John has to make (deciding which clothes to wear).

Mom said that one item of clothing that could cause issues for John was socks. Sometimes he needed to try a few pairs to find one that felt right. Knowing this helped us use the last plastic drawer for extra socks to give John a choice if he needed it.

Last, we set up a basket by the door with shoes for John. So if it is a morning that John is rushing, he can bring the shoes and socks in the car with him and finish that piece en route to school. We want to avoid a meltdown and give him a compromise by allowing him to finish the last few tasks in the car if needed.

If you feel that your sensory child would be motivated by a reward system when implementing a new system, you could create one for the first three weeks of the new system. Break down the reward system into a weekly timeframe for a more immediate reward. In this case, every

MIKE EGAN/EGAN IMAGES

A labeled plastic drawer unit.

day John is ready to go on time, he gets a sticker, and after five stickers he gets something special.

I checked in with John's mom a few weeks after setting up this new system and she reported that the morning rush had gotten much better and that they were getting out of the house with very few tears and almost no meltdowns. Sounds like a much better start to the day for everyone. It may sound like a bit of work to set up a system like this, but the improvement in daily living (happier children and less stress for parents) makes the time investment seem very small.

After-school Transition

Another common trouble time for sensory kids is the transition from school to home. As we know, they have been working hard all day to hold it together and have been navigating environments and situations that been frustrating and/or overwhelming to them. This will mean they will need a break and some structure to help them transition to home and get homework and dinner done successfully!

Again, if this is one of the toughest times of day for your sensory child, you may want to spend some time creating a specific schedule for this trouble time. By building in some play time, homework/break times, and some fascination exploration times, you can help this time of day run a little more smoothly. A picture/word schedule might look like this:

_______ Unpack backpack, Snack
_______ Active Playtime 20 to 30 minutes (swing, trampoline, tag outside)
_______ Homework
_______ Homework Break
_______ Homework
_______ Computer or TV Show, 30 minutes
_______ Dinner

For kids who are a little older, you may want to have them work with you to decide the order that they think works best for them. This may change day-to-day. Remember: don't get caught up in what you think the routine is "supposed to be." I worked with one sensory child who did his best work while moving so that meant reading while swinging, writing while standing on a disk seat, and reciting multiplication tables while walking around the house in a circle. The idea is to get to the same end point successfully, but with sensory kids, the path may be a little different. By being open to creative approaches and encouraging the fact that your sensory child is taking some ownership of what works for them, you will increase the likelihood of success.

Homework Plans. The *Leave It to Beaver* idea of kids coming home and going right up to their rooms to do homework is a Hollywood myth! Homework is another very common trouble time for many sensory kids, especially as they get older and must demonstrate more creative and interpretive thinking (something that is very hard for many sensory kids who view the world through a literal lens). Creating a very specific homework plan that is written daily on a whiteboard or on a visual schedule can help map out a plan of attack and provide a great visual checklist. Your sensory child may want to tackle the hardest things first with a break in between and save the best for last. Or she may want to do one hard task, one easy task, alternating until all of her homework is done. This plan of attack may change from day to day, depending on how flexible your child is feeling at that moment, so having a few homework plans on hand and giving your sensory child a choice can also be helpful.

Following is an example of a blank, laminated homework plan. This is something you would fill out daily with a dry-erase marker filling in the specific homework that will be done first, second, and third as well as specific break choices in between the homework times. An example of a homework plan might look like this:

HOMEWORK PLAN

homework

Homework ________________

breaktime

Break 10 minutes

homework

Homework ________________

breaktime

Break 10 minutes

homework

Homework ________________

The Picture Communication Symbols © 1981–2013 by Mayer-Johnson LLC. All Rights Reserved Worldwide. Used with permission. Boardmaker™ is a trademark of Mayer-Johnson LLC.

Here is an example of how this schedule might look like filled out:

HOMEWORK PLAN

homework

Homework *Math Questions 1—5 (hard)*

breaktime

Trampoline Break

homework

Homework *Math Questions 6—10 (hard)*

breaktime

Brain Break with Coloring

homework

Homework *Spelling Sheet, Complete all (easy)*

The Picture Communication Symbols © 1981–2013 by Mayer-Johnson LLC. All Rights Reserved Worldwide. Used with permission. Boardmaker™ is a trademark of Mayer-Johnson LLC.

Other Tools That Support Homework Time

Create a Few Homework Areas. Most likely, this will be out near you in the kitchen area or family room area until your child is older and more self-sufficient in managing homework. You may want to have two areas close to you that are not next to each other if you have two children doing homework at the same time. This allows you to support both kids at once without having them distracting each other. In addition, research shows that changing workstations on some rotating basis can increase productivity and focus for many kids. If your child has a tough time getting started, having a choice in homework location might help get them over the hump.

Create a Homework Bin or Plastic Drawer System for Each Child. These will have everything they need for homework: pencils, erasers, dictionary, paper, handheld sensory fidgets, disk seats, charts, and so on. The main goal is to not have your sensory child wandering around looking for items. Everything will be in one place. You want to keep them on task as best you can!

Tap into Some Noise (or Have No Noise). Noise-blocking headphones for sensory kids who are sensitive to auditory distractions will provide great support during homework time. Conversely, having an iPod or CD player with headphones with soft music on hand for our sensory kids that do well with distractions might help them stay on task.

Use Graphic Organizers. These are great tools for supporting different homework assignments. They are available for kids in grades kindergarten through third and fourth through eighth grades to make more visual some of the typical written academic assignments your child receives. These can give sensory kids a jumping-off point when having to do a creative or interpretive writing assignment or a word problem for math. Again, whenever you are able to "tell a story" in a visual format, you are creating something tangible that will help support your sensory child.

Try Different Techniques. You will need to experiment with different techniques to see when your sensory child is most engaged with homework. As mentioned, many sensory kids have difficulty doing two tasks at once, such as organizing thoughts and writing or typing them. See what happens when you type for your child and simply have him tell you what he wants to say on a particular writing assignment. You might be amazed to hear what your child produces when she can simply focus on one modality at a time. I've known some parents who have had great success teaching their older children to use voice-recognition software to assist with writing assignments. In either case, you let the child edit the writing so they are learning proper punctuation and grammar and get small doses of typing.

Chore Time

Chore time equals trouble time for many children. There are a few things to keep in mind during chore time for sensory kids. The main goal is that our sensory kids are contributing to the household and that they are successfully completing a task from start to finish. Think back to the Golden Tool: break it down, eliminate external and internal stimuli, and create a visual aid for support.

First, you want to break down the chores into manageable pieces. Instead of having your child clean their entire room, you can break the task into smaller parts that are easier for your child to get his head around. If the room has zones that are clearly labeled, you could assign him one zone a week to clean. You could also highlight the top two to three areas that are consistently a challenge and focus on those areas for chore times.

Next, you want to eliminate the distracting or interfering stimuli. This means no "help" from siblings! Pick a time of day or a day of the week that is usually quiet and calm for your child. For a child who is easily frustrated and sensitive to time constraints, save the more challenging chores for weekends, when there is more time to support a successful task.

Last, you need to create a visual aid. Take an index card and have a picture of how the completed chore should look on the front of the card. On the back, list the three-step process to get the chore done.

Here is an example of a "Clean your Bookcase" Chore Card. On the front of the card, we have a picture of the bookcase as it should look when the chore is complete (not too perfect here, but just how you could expect your sensory child to complete the chore). On the back, we have listed the three-step process to complete the chore:

CLEAN THE BOOKCASE CARD

1) Put all the big books on the bottom shelf.
2) Put all the medium and small books on the middle shelf.
3) Put all Pokémon card bins and Lego bins on the top shelf.

Again, the goal here is to have the task done successfully—not to have it look picture perfect. As your sensory child gets better at completing this chore, you can add additional steps to encourage and teach better categorizing and organization. The next version might look like this:

1. Put all the big books on the bottom shelf with the animal books on the left, the Percy Jackson books in the middle, and the mystery books on the right.

2. Put all the medium and small books on the middle shelf with all the chapter books on the right side and all the comic books on the left side.
3. Put all Pokémon card bins and Lego bins on the top shelf with the Pokémon bins on the right and the Lego bins on the left.

MIKE EGAN/EGAN IMAGES

A tidy bookcase.

Another way to support sensory kids during chore time is to do the first or hardest step for them. We know that many sensory kids struggle with executive function challenges. This means that the initial categorizing or planning for a task can be hard. If we can come up with a way to start a chore or begin the categorization process, that can sometimes be enough to get the chore started and completed successfully.

Let's use the example of laundry day. You want to begin to have your child sort and bring laundry to the washing machine for washing. He can bring dirty clothes from bedroom hampers into the bathroom, where you could have a three-bin system with each section labeled with words or pictures of colors (make sure you define what each "color category" means as that will not be a natural assumption for many sensory kids!):

- Whites (white, light gray, light pink, light blue)
- Medium Colors (dark gray, light blue, yellow, dark pink, purple)
- Darks (black, dark blue, red, dark green)

The visual on the wall above the laundry sorting system could read: "Once a bin is full, bring to the laundry area."

The Picture Communication Symbols © 1981–2013 by Mayer-Johnson LLC.
All Rights Reserved Worldwide. Used with permission. Boardmaker™ is a trademark of Mayer-Johnson LLC.

You have done the two things here to support a successful chore:

1. You have done the first step of the chore here (set up the wash color categories), which can be a help in getting distracted, disorganized, or overwhelmed kids started.
2. You have also eliminated one of the hardest parts of this process for many sensory kids: how to plan where to begin.

Connecting During a Tantrum

One of the most challenging trouble times for parents and sensory kids alike is the tantrum/explosive episode or meltdown. During these times, sensory kids are feeling out of control, misunderstood, and scared. Parents feel helpless and have no way to communicate, support, or calm their sensory child in this emotional place. Experiencing explosive tantrums can be emotional, heartbreaking, and draining for parents.

A few things that are helpful to remember about tantrums/explosive episodes/meltdowns:

Most important, know that you are not a bad parent. You may have inconsistent reactions (sometimes angry, sometimes sad, sometimes calm) to an explosive episode. This is no reflection on you as a parent. These episodes are hard to witness, and it can be very hard to know what to do as every episode can have a different trigger, last different lengths of time, and come at different times of day. Be patient with yourself as you learn to understand this process for your sensory child.

Tantrums serve an important purpose for many sensory kids. In younger sensory kids, tantrums can provide a much needed physical release after a long period of "holding it togther." They also give us the opportunity to begin to teach our sensory kids how to catch a feeling at the beginning and to learn more appropriate ways of expressing their feelings.

Tantrums also give us good information. You can pick up a lot of info about triggers and social challenges, as well as consistent times our sensory kids might be feeling misunderstood or overwhelmed. This allows us to be more proactive in preventing future meltdowns with better planning and support around certain experiences.

Tantrums give your child a safe way to "get it out and regroup." If you have taken some time to create a chill-out zone as mentioned in chapter 5, your child can go there and begin to calm down. Your calm reaction will let him know that this is okay, and even expected on some level, which removes some of the negative feelings associated with a tantrum.

Our sensory kids feel out of control and scared when they are having a tantrum, explosive episode, or meltdown and may need some help in reconnecting with others and/grounding themselves right after an episode. In addition, siblings may feel scared when they see a brother or sister have an explosive episode. It is extremely important that siblings feel safe and secure. During a calm period, talk with typical siblings about your sensory child. Come up with some language to use when discussing tantrums and explaining why they happen, and what helps their brother or sister calm down. You can also get sibling support for this piece by working with a therapist or psychologist who understands your sensory child's profile and how to support typical siblings.

We know how helpful simple picture schedules and word schedules can be for our sensory kids for setting daily expectations and supporting them during transitions. This is especially true during or right after a tantrum, explosive episode, or meltdown. This is a time that our sensory kids will be very disconnected and internalized, they will be unable to navigate what is okay/not okay, and it will be next to impossible to communicate with them at this time. They also might feel very badly about themselves after an explosive episode and might need your help in "normalizing" their experience and feelings.

Creating a picture or word schedule to support a meltdown or tantrum can be a very effective way to offer some support, provide them with a few choices about how to calm down, and remove the human element (you!). Be sure to incorporate something that falls into a current fascination as that will be instantly calming. You can also invite them to come find you when they are ready so you are not touching or hugging them before they are fully regulated. Lastly, be mindful of how badly some sensory kids feel about themselves after a tantrum and add something at the end about how great they are/how much you love them. You could create a "How to Calm Down" schedule with or without the help of your child. The schedule would be reviewed with your sensory child at a time of day your child is the most calm and connected. The "How to Calm Down" schedule could be posted in the chill-out zone or in the Central Message Area to allow your child to easily access it visually when needed. You might have a picture or word schedule look like this:

The Picture Communication Symbols © 1981–2013 by Mayer-Johnson LLC. All Rights Reserved Worldwide. Used with permission. Boardmaker™ is a trademark of Mayer-Johnson LLC.

Sometimes, you may find that your sensory child wants nothing to do with a "How to Calm Down" schedule and just needs to go cry or stomp it out somewhere. Again, as long as they are safe and the people around them are safe, try to let them get it out. What has worked well with a few of my clients who deal with explosive episodes is to write a note on a piece of paper and slide it under the bedroom door. This works well for older sensory kids as you are giving them the space to experience their feelings but offering them a small amount of support specific to this one situation without being in their face. The trick is waiting until you hear them entering into a calmer phase and taking that opportunity to slide a note under the door that says, "You are such a great kid with great feelings. If you are confused about what happened, I can help you figure it out when you are ready." Some older sensory kids will do well writing notes back and forth to a parent after an explosive episode—this can be a safer way for them to communicate until they are calm and connected again.

Explosive Note Writing Technique

Dad and Beth were doing Beth's homework together and were working on math, which was extremely frustrating for Beth. She was getting more and more rigid and snappy with Dad during homework time despite breaks. It finally got to the point where she made a mistake and had a complete meltdown. She was yelling, screaming, and trying to hit Dad. He moved her back to her room to try to get her to her chill-out area but she kept coming out. After the third time, she managed to stay in her room and after ten minutes of crying and yelling she started to calm down. Then it seemed like she found one of her favorite books and was reading. Dad took this opportunity to write this note to Beth and put it under her door.

Beth,

You are a very smart girl and we love you very much. We know that math sometimes feels hard for you (this is also true for many other kids!). We are on your side and will work with you to make sure you understand how to do your math homework. Here are a few ideas I have we can try:

Dad can do the first problem with you and show you how I got the answer step-by-step.

To make our math time go a little faster, we could do either just the even numbers or the odd numbers on your math homework.

We could review five minutes of our favorite math computer game to see if that helps us remember the math rules in your homework.

We could review the math lesson on YouTube and see if that helps us remember the math rules in your homework

Think about it and when you are ready, come out and let me know what idea you think is the best one.

Love,
Dad

Why this helped Beth:

- She read that her parents love her even after a big meltdown.
- It normalized her feelings about being frustrated with math.
- Dad created some options for tackling the math but gave Beth the final choice.
- Beth was invited to come out when she was calm.

It is also important to be realistic about explosive episodes. They are hard on parents, siblings, and sensory kids. One of the main goals of the systems, routines, and structure in this book is to make our kids feel safer, happier, and less anxious. This should reduce the frequency and intensity of explosive episodes. Employing the techniques in this section will help you and your sensory child manage through explosive episodes when they happen, but there is no magic bullet. At the same level, we have to do our best to detach ourselves emotionally, fight our own frustration, and provide a calm, supportive environment for everyone. Being calm in the midst of an explosive episode does not add fuel to the fire and can be great modeling for all of our kids.

Unstructured Times: Creating Structure When None Exists

As we mentioned earlier, most sensory kids do better during times of structure and predictability with some built-in downtime. This means that the times of year that have no schedule—like summer or school vacations—or times that have many new activities added to the normal schedule—like holidays—are going to be challenging for sensory kids. But there are some strategies you can use to support these unstructured and sometimes overwhelming times.

The Long Summer

We all look forward to lazy summer days when the schedule is loose and school-time routines fade away. Some downtime is imperative for all of us, but for sensory kids, the loose schedules can mean unpredictable days and worsen some of their behavior. But changes in your normal routines and schedules don't have to throw your family for a loop. Here are a few things to try at home over the summer to create some structure during the downtime:

Adjust the Central Message Area. Even though school is over, we still need to write out what is coming for the week. Include camps, beach trips or pool outings, when there will be downtime at home, reading time, as well as some of the daily expectations. Letting your child know what is happening and when to expect it can lower his anxiety level and prepare him for the times he will need to be engaged.

Build in a Loose Routine. Have some things that you expect your child to do every day, and include them on the Central Message Area. A chore or two, some reading and math time, and snacks are all things that can be included to create a schedule. You can also add a few things that you do on the same night every week, like dessert is ice cream on Wednesdays and popsicles on Fridays.

Differentiate the Summer Week and the Summer Weekend. This will help younger kids understand time/calendar during the summer months. For example, Mom and Dad still work during the week and are home on the weekends. Come up with a list of things you can do on sunny and rainy weekdays during the summer and hang them in your Central Message Area. Then create a separate list of special things that will be done on the summer weekends. These supports will help all kids understand the concept of time over the summer and will help them feel more grounded and organized.

Week On/Week Off. For kids who do much better with routine, consider supporting them with a week on/week off camp routine, or build in activities that are somewhat regular and structured throughout the summer. The structured activity can support a few different types of sensory kids. For the child who has a high activity level and needs to be active, the structured activities will support these needs. Also, for the child who can be withdrawn and not engaged socially, these structured activities can engage him cognitively and support social connections. As an extra bonus, allow him to pick one activity that supports one of his fascinations like chess, or make your own computer game camp.

Make Summer Learning Fun. Summer is a great time to embrace those multisensory learning opportunities, such as making or tending a garden or creating a wooden float that will work in the pool. Another great multisensory learning tool is the diorama. This can be a fun research project to do over the summer. Let your child pick the topic (another good way to let your child tap into his or her fascination) or it can relate to a family trip you are taking over the summer as a fun preparation. Let her decide how she wants to research it (library, computer, or both) and what materials she wants to use to create her diorama.

Join Summer Reading Clubs. Keeping the routine with a fun, structured reading program that has a reward at the end is bound to be a success for most children. If your child needs a more structured routine, consider getting him some regular tutoring to help them maintain and build learning skills over the summer in a more organized way.

Organizing 101. Take the extra time you have with your child over the summer to teach simple organizing skills. Since we all have a little extra time during the summer, this can be a great time to have your sensory child learn a new task. Maybe your child could start to pack his own lunch for camp/beach trips. You could give him the two or three easy pieces of the task like getting the drink, snack, and fruit and save the harder piece, making the sandwich, for you.

Get a Head Start on the School Routine. Prepare for the school routine before school starts. Three weeks is the magic number for helping your kids successfully readjust to a new sleeping schedule or routine. Start by setting bedtime fifteen minutes earlier each night and getting up fifteen minutes earlier until you reach the target school sleep/wake schedule. Start going to the school playground to play, which is a simple, fun way to refamiliarize your child with one part of their school. Create a booklet if your child seems particularly anxious about a new grade change, and start reviewing a typical school day in the new grade. If a new morning schedule is something the child is expected to do independently at school, create that laminated checklist for them to review before school starts (see chapter 8).

Set up your summer to be relaxing but predictable by preparing your sensory child and creating a summer schedule. By adjusting the Central Message Area, building in loose routines, and teaching a new organizing skill or task, you will have the tools in place to have a summer balanced with routines and relaxation!

Holiday Breaks

For most children, Halloween kicks off the start of their favorite two months of the year: the holidays! For sensory kids, this can be a time of year filled with uncomfortable experiences such as changes in routines, relatives and friends visiting, and lots of additional social interactions. This time of year is filled with a chaotic energy that is almost palpable for some kids. It is important to identify the situations that will be difficult for your child during this time of year. This will allow you to create a few simple ways to provide extra support during the holidays.

Preparing for Changes in Routines. Preparing your sensory child for what is coming is one way to support them in their day-to-day experiences all year round. This is especially true this time of year, when there are frequent changes in their regular schedule. Create a visual support whenever possible before a change is coming. Explain in pictures and/or words the new schedule, making sure to highlight what they have done before successfully or people they will see whom they enjoy.

Make sure to include a few options of what can be done when your child is overwhelmed or needs a break.

Visits and Interactions with New People. Spontaneous visits can happen frequently this time of year. Try to set the expectation of more visits and social interactions. For younger sensory kids, try making a story about "People We See Over the Holidays." You can also talk about the social expectations of these visits in the book: saying "hi" and introducing yourself to the visitor, for example. For older sensory kids, make a laminated sheet that explains what you expect them to do socially with visitors, how long they need to stay and "visit" and when they can go do their own thing. (For more on Situation Cards, see chapter 10.)

Make Holiday Travel Easier. Again, preparation ahead of time is key to making holiday travel easy on yourself, your family, and your sensory child. Give your sensory child a visual of where you are going via online sites, pictures of the family home where you will be visiting, and images of the people you will be seeing. For younger sensory kids, make a trip book that explains what will happen during your travels. During your visit, set up a space for your child that is their "escape and regulate" spot. It can hold the toys or things that are calming and relaxing, and can be as simple as a bag of favorite books, arts and crafts, or action figures in a quiet bedroom. For more detailed information on traveling with sensory kids, see chapter 11.

Is It a "Must Do" for Your Sensory Child? Take stock of the upcoming holiday events and create a list of "Must Do's" for your sensory child. Some events may be extra challenging for them, and there might be one or two events that they could skip. Could they just stay at home with a babysitter or go to a friend's house rather than attend a neighbor's holiday potluck? Sometimes skipping one party will give a sensory child the necessary downtime to make the next event a bit more relaxing and enjoyable for everyone.

Make a conscious effort to take some of the stress out of the holidays for you. Create a few simple supports to prepare them for new routines, to set expectations for frequent visitors and more social interactions, and to make holiday travel easier.

I hope that you now have some better tools to use to help your sensory child during dreaded tasks and/or unstructured time. When you tap into the Power of Choice, the Art of Distraction, and the Gift of the Fascination, you can support your sensory child in so many ways during those uncomfortable times. Having Sensory Organizing plans in place around the morning rush, homework time, and long summer days can be a great tool for helping our sensory kids get over the hump, complete tasks successfully, and manage looser routines. Now it's time to take these same Sensory Organizing concepts and apply them to our sensory child's experiences outside of the home.

Part 3

Helping Your Sensory Child in the World

Chapter 10

Leaving the Nest

Preparing Your Sensory Child for Challenging Situations

We have learned some great strategies for supporting our sensory kids at home, which will help make our time together more productive and peaceful. Now we need to take some of these same principles and apply them to your sensory child's out-of-home experiences. These out-of-home experiences give us great information about their strengths and challenges, and they give us wonderful teaching opportunities to help our sensory child develop confidence, social skills, and tangible tools for successful experiences.

As adults, we prepare ourselves for out-of-home experiences all the time. Let's say you are going to a dinner party. You find out what the dress code is, which gives you some immediate information about the event. You also find out who will be there; this gives you information about whom you might talk to, what you might talk about, and whom you are excited to see. You sometimes have even more information such as what will be on the menu, how long the dinner party will be, and how long the drive is to get there. When you get into the car with your partner for the event, you might review names of people we will be seeing, their careers and family information, and common interests. This is all information that helps us prepare for the situation, the social exchanges we might have while we are there, and how long we have to be connected and engaged.

We need to do some of these same things for our sensory kids when we are preparing them for a new, overwhelming, or stressful situation outside of the home. They need to have a map of what to expect, whom they might see, when they might get to do a desired activity, and how they can take a break if they need one.

In this chapter, we are going to learn how to identify overwhelming situations, prepare our sensory child ahead of time, and have a few supports in place during the experience. We will also look at the social piece and how simple tools will help support a social challenge as well as set expectations around a social situation. Finally, we will learn to highlight the successes and learn from the mistakes.

Identifying Overwhelming Situations

Let's start by getting a solid understanding of your sensory child and what some of the situational and social triggers are outside of the home. This first step will help us begin to anticipate situations that might be stressful and overwhelming to them. This can be one of those times where it might be helpful to pull out and review the SSK Sensory Organizing Worksheet and answer the same questions based on experiences outside the home only. I have changed the order of some of the questions and adjusted some of the wording to reflect out-of-the-home experiences.

To Identify Triggers and Challenges, Consider:

- What are some of the main challenges your child lives with day-to-day? Are issues related to anxiety, rigidity, and/or attentional issues? Are the same challenges present during experiences outside of the home, or do new challenges come up? For example, is he nervous about trying new things, does he get stuck on one way to do or experience something, does he have a hard time settling down and engaging when in a new or uncomfortable situation?

- Do you see any sensory tendencies in your child? What do the sensory tendencies look like outside of the home? Is she overwhelmed by loud noises, bright lights, tight or crowded places, too much visual stimuli, or strong smells?
- What are your child's strengths and things he loves to do? What does he love to do with other kids? What are favorite places to visit? Which activities connect and engage your child?
- What are the three biggest current challenges for your child that impact life experiences outside the home?
- What are common triggers for your child (things that get him upset, anxious, or overwhelmed)? Think of sensory and social triggers that might be more prevalent during experiences outside of the home.
- Does your child have difficulty with transitions? If so, what transitions typically cause the most anxiety/disruption?
- What are the most common current social experiences for your sensory child: play dates with lots of kids and parents, play dates at individual friends' houses, birthday parties, group outings with some friends, family get-togethers, outings with a few families, and so on.

To Plan for the Experience and Help Support Your Child There, Consider:

- How does your child process information and learn? Visual, auditory, or tactile/kinesthetic? This will help you prepare a few ways to present information about new experiences. Remember: we always want to include some sort of visual format.
- How does your child calm down when upset? Are there some ways your child will be able to do some of these things during the new experience?
- What are your child's strengths and things they are good at and love to do? How can you incorporate some of these things into the new experience or the portable chill-out zone you create?
- Does your child have a favorite color, character, or fascination? Again, can you tie some of these things into the experience to help

calm and connect your sensory child or ease him into the new environment?

If you spend some time answering these questions after challenging experiences outside of the home, you will have valuable information about common triggers, social challenges, as well as ways your sensory child will connect outside of the home. This will allow you to take the next steps in creating tangible, visual supports.

Some Common Stressful Situations

To help us get into the mind of a sensory child, let's review some of the more common overwhelming situations and why they might impact your child. Often, having a real understanding of why something is a challenge can help us create a plan or support that gets right to the level that speaks to them.

Dentist. I'm not sure I need to explain why this is a challenge (think of the loud noises, drills, funny smells, and new tastes and textures with cleaning pastes and polishes). This is hard for almost *every* child, and many adults, too!

Doctors. Again, lots of new, unexpected sensory input here, and sometimes your child is sick, to boot.

Birthday or Family Parties. This can be one of the hardest situations for parents. We parents have a preconceived idea that you can bring your kids to a birthday party or a cookout and let them go and have fun. There are new toys, lots of kids, so it should be great, right? Nothing to worry about! Well, as most sensory parents soon realize, this is a situation that can be very challenging for kids and their families.

Anything with a Crowd. Loud noises, people you don't know pushing into you, new sights and smells. Add in the fear of losing Mom and Dad in the crowd, and a sensory kid can't find anything calming or normal anywhere about them.

Concerts. See "Anything with a Crowd" and add extremely loud music to it!

Grocery or Clothes Shopping. Big building with lots of fluorescent lights, food or clothes stacked up to the ceiling—a sensory kid doesn't know what to look at or touch first. A kid is asked to put food that smells funny into shopping carts, or to try on clothes that smell funny, feel itchy, and have fifteen tags on them. All your sensory kid wants to do is go to his quiet place and read.

Restaurants. Your child has to sit in the same chair for a long time and is not allowed to move around. They don't make her favorite food here, and she's supposed to tell a stranger what she wants to eat (and that stranger is looking at her funny). When her food arrives, it smells funny and it does not taste like the way Mom makes it.

Anything New. In a new situation, your child has no map for what to expect at all. He has no idea where he is going or what he is doing. *Will I be able to play video games? Will anyone there like me? Will Mom and Dad be with me? What if I hate it there—am I stuck there?* Questions can go on and on with this one!

Common Overwhelming and Stressful Situations by Sensory Profile

Since we are supporting many different types of sensory kids—and sometimes kids who have overlapping profiles—let's review some of the common sensory profiles and why new or overwhelming situations might be stressful for all types of kids.

Sensory Kids with Attention Challenges. A new or overwhelming experience can require lots of information to learn or recall in order to be successful and socially connected. For example, a child with attention challenges will walk into a birthday party not sure where to look or what to do first: say hi to her friends or meet some of the new kids, go jump on the bounce house, go get a handful of snacks, or go run around outside. She may present as a buzzing bee bouncing around the party and never settling enough to complete an activity or be fully engaged with friends.

Sensory Kids Who Are Rigid or Inflexible. These children will be unsure of what to expect in new situations—they are not always comfortable navigating the "flow" of activities (moving from one activity to another), and they can have a tough time formulating appropriate responses to what's happening in the moment. They do not have a "map" of what to expect in unfamiliar situations. They can also get stuck on one way for an experience to unfold so the natural ebb and flow of everyday experiences can be overwhelming. The rigid sensory child may get to the party and want to have the cake first or get hyperfocused on one desired activity and may have a hard time letting others participate or moving on to other things.

Sensory Kids Who Are Overwhelmed and/or Anxious. They can a have a natural fear of the unknown or unexpected. They also can remember and hyperfocus on detailed pieces of a past experience that they did not like or that made them uncomfortable. They may not like the new people, loud noises, or games at birthday parties, so they may be slow to engage or may hang back with a parent as they try to understand what is going on around them.

Sensory Kids Who Have Social Challenges. They can have inherent challenges with the social nuances that go on at any social event, especially if it is unstructured (for example, a big family cookout or a group play date). While a birthday party may have some structure to how it unfolds, the sensory child with social challenges may be overwhelmed with the number of other kids present and retreat. They also may have a hard time with some of the social rules at a birthday party. For example, that the birthday child gets to be first in line for all of the party activities or gets to have the first piece of cake may not make sense to kids who have problems understanding or accepting the social rules—and their exceptions—in a particular setting.

Sensory Kids Who Have Executive Function Deficits. They can have a hard time with the planning, sequencing, and organization needed to prepare for and understand the flow of a situation. For a birthday party, they might forget to make a birthday card for their friend or have a hard time learning new games that might be played there. Also, they may not understand the expectation of standing near and singing to the birthday child during cake time and might wander off to check something else out.

If you add sensory sensitivities (loud noises, strong smells, sensitive to visual stimuli, uncomfortable in big crowds) to any of the above profiles, you have the recipe for one overwhelmed child. Also, as we mentioned before, many sensory kids that we are supporting have a blend of a few of these profiles, so we need techniques that will help a broad range of challenges for many different types of situations.

Preparing for Overwhelming Situations

Thankfully, as we found with many of our at home supports, most of the same techniques will work to support all of these sensory profiles outside the home. Preparing ahead of time, having a few contingency plans in place, learning your child's "overwhelmed" and "need a break" signals, and having a list of things your sensory child can do to "escape"—for a few moments or for good—go a long way toward avoiding and coping with these challenging moments.

Hop Online. Before you go out for a new experience, see what you can find online to prepare your child. Say you are going to a birthday party at a Chuck E. Cheese's. You could go to the Chuck E. Cheese website and show your child pictures of Chuck E. Cheese, the games on site, and the party room. You could also watch videos on the Chuck E.

Cheese site that show a birthday party in progress. Look at a menu to see if there is a favorite food or a favorite game on site your child can look forward to. For extra support, you could take a quick field trip to Chuck E. Cheese a week before the event.

Role Play or Act It Out at Home. Create your own version of the experience at home. This will allow you to practice the experience in your own way before it happens. If we stick with the Chuck E. Cheese example, you could set up a pretend party room in your play area with a few electronic games or ball games. You could play some loud music and let your child play a few games before it's time for the birthday pizza dinner.

Read or Create Your Own Social Experience Stories. Make a Chuck E. Cheese Birthday Party Book. You could print out a few pictures from the Chuck E. Cheese website and make a small book in sequential order.

Page 1: Picture of Chuck E. Cheese and picture and/or name of birthday child
Page 2: Picture of games at Chuck E. Cheese's
Page 3: Picture of party room for pizza, cake, and presents
Page 4: Picture of saying good-bye to birthday child

Apps for Tablets, Smart Phones, and Laptops. There are so many wonderful social tools and supports available for iPhones, iPads, and other devices. Here are a few popular sites and apps, but there are more being created all the time!

- Model Me Kids: Model Me Kids has apps for iPhone, iPod Touch, iPad, and Droid. These are great visual tools in a slideshow format of children during common experiences outside of the home: playground, haircut, restaurant, mall, and so on. www.modelmekids.com/iphone-app-autism.html.

- Proloquo2Go: This is a communication program for kids who have difficulty speaking, won't communicate vocally when they are overwhelmed, or have a hard time expressing their feelings. The program offers symbols for many common experiences. Apps for iPhone, iPod Touch, and iPad are available: www.proloquo2go.com.

Prepare a Portable Chill Zone or Break Spot. Know that despite great preparation, there is a high probability that your sensory child will need a break during the experience. Prepare a portable chill zone or break spot that you can have in the car or have with you to set up in a quiet room at the location. Things to include: favorite books, toys, games, sensory handheld toys, portable music with headphones, favorite food treat. When you see your child showing signs of being overwhelmed or checking out, bring him or her to the portable chill zone for a short time. Be prepared with some options to help them navigate the challenge of re-engaging to the party activity. You might let them pick a favorite handheld toy from the chill zone to bring with them, or give them the option of watching the activity for two minutes before joining in.

How to Support Your Child During the Overwhelming Experience

Get ready, get set, go! Now that you are on your way, here are a few simple ideas to keep in mind as you get to, and begin to enjoy, the party.

Timing Is Everything. One simple way to set up our sensory kids to be successful is to be one of the early birds at the party. This allows them to come in without a big crowd, gives them some time to case out the joint and find some things of interest, and allows them to get comfortable with a few kids before the rest of the guests arrive.

On the flipside, when the party has been running at full steam, dinner is done, and kids are getting tired, this is a good time to gather your crew and leave on a positive note. This is the time that roughhousing starts, kids start getting antsy, and signals get crossed. Being one of the first ones to leave allows your sensory child to leave on a good note, which is a great confidence builder for future parties.

Know Your Child's Signals. Come to the party with a solid understanding of your child's verbal, nonverbal, behavioral, and physical signs that they are overwhelmed. Some sensory kids may have a hard time recognizing and/or telling us when they need a break. Children who need a break might:

- disengage from the group and be off by themselves
- be louder and more out of control than the rest of the kids
- hyperfocus on one activity, one person, or one game
- have a hard time or resist switching from activity to activity
- suddenly become extremely tired
- say things like "This party is stupid" or "Everyone thinks I'm weird"
- become extremely silly and unable to stop
- begin to use verbal aggression, threats, and/or respond in a physically aggressive way toward others.

These may all be indications that your sensory child needs a break. A break can be a visit to the portable chill zone in the car, a visit to a quiet room in the house with a few favorite books, toys, or a handheld video game, or some time outside doing something physical to get a release (trampoline, shooting baskets, scooter ride, and so on). If after a break, your child continues to show signs of stress, it might be time to leave the party.

Tap into the Art of Distraction, the Power of Choice, and the Gift of the Fascination

Some other great tools to tap into during an overwhelming situation are a few we talked about in chapter 9: the art of distraction, the power of choice, and the gift of the fascination. All of these can redirect sensory kids when they are overwhelmed, give them some control when they are feeling out of control, and give them a way to connect to new friends and a new place. Let's work with our party example to demonstrate these techniques:

The Art of Distraction. Redirect your child to a fun toy at the party. This lets your child focus on the toy instead of the number of new people in the room and can be a soft way to transition them into the situation.

The Power of Choice. Give your child a choice to get her engaged socially (be sure to give two choices you know your child will be interested in, but avoid more than that, which can be overwhelming). For example, "What would you like to do first? Do you want to go on the trampoline or go play a board game with Anne?"

The Gift of the Fascination. When your child hits a trouble spot and seems overwhelmed or disengaged, pull in their fascination. For example, "Anne has a SpongeBob book she said you could read. Let's go find you a quiet spot where you can take a look at this."

What Behavior Can Teach You

Many times, our sensory kids will use behavior to show their frustration, confusion, and anxiety about a new experience. This may happen before the overwhelming experience or after something unexpected or upsetting has happened to them during it. They may get rigid or explosive, they may latch on to a rule associated with the new experience as being something they can't live with, or they may say no one likes or wants to play with them. They also may pick a small thing to control about the upcoming situation as a way to feel a sense of order about what is coming. These are all ways of asking for help. These behaviors may be worse with unexpected transitions or transitions to unknown or undesired activities. If you know that behavior can be a way your sensory child asks for help, you can disconnect from the behavior and focus on the strategy your child needs.

Here's one example of how this might work in a typical situation. Mike is going on a group hike with his family. Due to time constraints, the family did not have a lot of time to prepare Mike for the experience beforehand. Mike had a rough transition and latched on to one rule that he did not want to abide by: sneakers must be worn on the hike. Because Mike has sensory challenges, he prefers loose shoes like Crocs.

Mom and Dad brought both the sneakers and Crocs, knowing that some negotiating would occur. They recognized Mike's behavior as transition anxiety. When they arrived at the trail head, Mike was still hyperfocused on the shoe rule. Dad went on to the meet the guide at the start of the trail with Mike's siblings while Mom stayed to negotiate with Mike. She compromised with Mike by saying he could wear his Crocs but that she would have to pack the sneakers in the backpack just in case. When Mike still was having a hard time, she also did a smart thing and gave Mike an out. She had already agreed with Dad that if Mike couldn't let go of his hyperfocus on the rule, she and Mike would skip the hiking trip. She said to Mike, "If the shoe situation is too much for you, we can skip the trip and wait here for the others." This did two things:

1. It gave Mike an out, which relieved the tension around the "I have to do this" feeling; and
2. She broke Mike's hyperfocus on the shoe rule. Now it was not about the shoe rule. It was about whether or not Mike wanted to go on the hiking trip with his family. In this case, this proved to be enough for Mike to pull it together and after a small adjustment period, have a great time on the trip.

Now this can go the other way sometimes, and Mom and Mike might have needed to skip the trip and wait for the others to come back, which is also okay. This type of experience can give you information about how you might do it differently next time: more preparation for Mike before the hiking outing, a map of the trail for Mike to bring to review, a scavenger hunt for things to find on the trail, and any other strategies to get Mike connected to the experience and not sidetracked by his anxiety.

Now that we have identified the overwhelming situations and come up with strategies to prepare and support our sensory child during these situations, we can begin to look at the social experiences that are going on during these situations and provide some supports for those. The social piece can be a big part of why our sensory kids feel overwhelmed and/or disconnected in many situations. Simple tools and mini social skill trainings can help our sensory kids feel more confident in how to interact in different settings.

Navigating Social Situations

Some of the harder pieces to anticipate when preparing for out-of-home experiences are the social challenges that might arise for your sensory child. These can vary from experience to experience and can be specific to age or the number of kids in a group, as well as where your sensory child is developmentally and how he is feeling that day. We want to do what we can to anticipate the social interactions that will be hard for our children and give them a few simple social tools to help them better understand the social experiences that might be coming.

Again, first we want to identify the social situations our sensory kids are exposed to currently. This might be a good time to look back on the SSK Sensory Organizing Worksheet we reviewed at the beginning of this chapter. The seventh question gives us a quick way to identify social situations: "What are the current social experiences for your sensory child—play dates with lots of kids and parents, play dates at individual friends' houses, birthday parties, group outings with some friends, family get-togethers, outings with a few families, etc.?" When you have a basic list of what the common social interactions are for your sensory child, you can begin to address the possible social needs.

Party Plan for Parents

Part of supporting your sensory child's experience is adjusting your own expectations for your child's behavior in a party situation. Here are a few tips for shifting into the new sensory party experience:

- Reset your own expectations about the experience.
- Before you go, review the current key triggers or challenges for your sensory child with your partner.
- Take turns with your partner: one of you socialize, while the other keeps tabs on your child, then at a specific time, you switch.
- Even though everyone else might be doing it, think twice about leaving your sensory child at a "drop-off" birthday party.
- Be prepared to address comments you might get from other parents suggesting you are "too overprotective" or you can leave as "everything will be fine." Some responses might be "Parties can be hard for Sarah—they always seem to run more smoothly when one of us can stick around to help if needed" or something more neutral like "I love having the opportunity to see the kids hang out and play together."
- Check in with any typical siblings. Make sure they are not "taking care" of their sensory sibling as this is a chance for them to socialize freely, also.
- Always consider having two cars or arranging for an alternate ride home for your partner and typical kids in case you need to leave early with your sensory child.

What Are the Situational Social Challenges for Your Sensory Child?

The next piece in the social puzzle is understanding what the core social challenges are for your child in different situations. This may take some observation on your part in different situations. Watch and take objective notes (or ask trusted teachers, family, or friends to do this for you) on what some of their natural tendencies are during social interactions, as well as what is working and what is a struggle. Whoever is taking notes will be looking for information that answers these questions for each situation.

- When does your child seem most connected and relaxed?
- Does your child have a hard time understanding the normal back-and-forth process of conversation?
- Does your child say things that don't fit into the conversation?
- Does your child leave a room when too many kids are around, or does he hang around the periphery and try to find a way to get into the mix?
- Does your child naturally seek out someone who has common interests, or does he need help with that?
- How does your child react when he feels misunderstood? Does he react physically or does he disengage from the group?

Having some of the real-life information at your fingertips can really help you create a social tool that is relevant and meaningful to your child. This is all great information to help them find the balance of a successful social situation.

Understanding the Subtle Social Challenges

One of the harder pieces to understand are challenges our sensory kids might have in the subtle social exchanges and/or subtle social rules. Many times, this is a part of the exchange we do on autopilot and never have had to think about. For many of our sensory kids with autism, Asperger's, AD/HD, anxiety disorder, or SPD, understanding these kinds of social cues is not automatic and can be a very difficult and overwhelming part of communicating with others. They are constantly trying to read what a look or movement might mean while also trying to hear our words, never fully understanding how both pieces work together. This alone will have our sensory kids on edge in many situations.

They can also have a hard time generalizing information from one experience and applying the information learned to future similar experiences. They often are not able to pull information from one social exchange and use that to prepare for the next similar social exchange. This is where some of the many social tools out there can help. You can tap into a variety of resources to help teach your sensory child some social rules: "feelings" charts that help your child rate their feelings in response to certain situations, stories or booklets that you can create for your sensory child about "How to Make Friends" and other topics, and flashcards of common facial expressions and feelings with a picture, label, and description are all ways of teaching some of the possible exchanges in social interactions. (See "Products I Love" at the back of the book.)

The much harder pieces to teach are the social nuances. There are many, many social nuances and they can be complicated to anticipate and hard to explain. A few examples of social nuances your sensory child might be struggling with include:

- How do I understand when someone does something by accident or on purpose to me?
- How do I know when I am getting in someone's social space and they are uncomfortable?
- How do I know when someone is teasing me in a mean way or a fun way?
- How do I know when someone is done talking to me and is ready to go talk or play with someone else?
- Why it is not okay to say certain things (for example, exactly what I am thinking without a filter)?
- How do I know when it is okay to start talking to someone? Do they look at me a certain way?
- How do I know when someone is tired of listening to what I am talking about?
- What do I do when someone says something mean to me?

If you have some ideas of what social nuances are difficult for your sensory child, you can create a personalized tool to help your child develop a social plan of attack. This not only builds confidence, but it also helps them understand the process of asking "why" when they do not understand a social exchange or situation.

Social Tools

One of the great social teachers out there is Michelle Garcia Winner, who developed the acclaimed Social Thinking Program (visit www.socialthinking.com). Michelle focuses on helping parents understand the social thinking process, thus helping parents get to their child's core social thinking challenges. This helps parents create the right supports for teaching social lessons. She offers workshops for parents and teachers as well as many books and DVDs for children, teens, and adults who need support with social thinking. Some of her most popular books include *You Are a Social Detective*, presented in a comic book format for kids, and *Superflex: A Superhero Social Thinking Curriculum Package*, the latter being a popular program for teachers, educators, and parents supporting all types of sensory kids with social challenges. Additional information is listed in the Resources section.

Create Your Own Situation Cards. Now that we have identified the top two or three social challenges in different situations as well as a few social nuances, we can create some specific tools for each of these experiences. One tool you can use is a visual aid I like to call the Situation Card. These can be made for each situational social challenge and each social nuance you want to assist your child in learning. This allows you to make it detailed and personal, relevant to what your child is struggling with now, and allows you to suggest choices that work for your child. Your Situation Card can include typed or handwritten text and drawn pictures or images taken from photographs and other sources. You can laminate them and keep them at home or in the car for easy review on the way to the social event.

Following are two examples of Social Experience Cards. As mentioned, the party is a situation that many sensory kids have a hard time navigating. With these cards, we are going to include information about why parties are fun, why parties can be overwhelming, how to recognize when you need a break, and what options are available to prevent aggressive behavior or a complete shutdown. Also, since we mentioned that they can have a tough time generalizing from one situation to another, having this on hand for each party situation can prepare them for the next party before they arrive. Lastly, we are giving them information in a concrete, literal way without parental involvement, which means less emotion and better processing, memory, and recall. If your child can read, it's best to let her read it quietly (resist the urge to try to explain it) and then ask if she has any questions.

Situation Card Party Plan

Parties are fun and you can have a great time! But at times, parties can be overwhelming for all of us because sometimes we are in a new place, it can be noisy, and there are new people playing different games that can be hard to understand.

<u>So it's important to know when it's time for a break at a party. Some signs you might need a break:</u>

1. You are feeling like "this is the worst party ever" or "no one understands me."
2. You feel really tired all of a sudden or you are getting frustrated with the changes or rules in the games being played.
3. You feel like you are on the verge of getting angry or having a meltdown. <u>Find Mom, Dad, or another adult that you know and say you need a break.</u>

What You Can Do for a Break

1. Go find a book to read in a quiet place in the house.
2. Go play Wii or DSi by yourself in a quiet place in the house for 10 to 15 minutes.
3. Ask Mom or Dad to take you home. It's okay to decide that you are done with the party.

What You Can Never Do!!!

Call anyone names.

Hit or kick anyone for any reason. If you are confused about something that happened, come find Mom or Dad to explain.

Next, we have an example of a Social Nuance Card. Again, we are going to target a specific social nuance that we know our sensory child is not understanding. We are going to label the card based on the nuance we are explaining, give clues to look for to get information on what is happening (expressions we might see, what someone might say, and how they might react immediately after the event). We will also provide what can never be done.

Social Nuance Card:
Did Someone Do Something by Accident or on Purpose?

Sometimes people do things to us by accident, and sometimes people do something to us on purpose. It can be hard to tell the difference. We don't want to assume that someone did something on purpose because, most often, something has been done by accident.

First, we need to look at some clues that can tell us how someone might look and act if they do something to us by accident.

1. Usually they are just doing something normal like walking along, playing, or running, and they lose track of where their body is and hit us with their hand, leg, foot, arm, or body.
2. They might have a surprised, shocked, or blank look on their face because what just happened was a surprise for them too. Some looks they might have are: (here it may be helpful to insert a few facial expressions as a visual).
3. After it happens, they might:

   Reach out their hand to touch us and say "sorry" immediately.

Feel embarrassed and look down and mumble "sorry."

Not know what to say because they are so surprised at what happened.

If one of these three things happens, we can probably assume that something was done by accident.

Always stop, look for clues, and ask the person what happened. "Hey, why did you do that?" Many times people will answer, "I'm sorry, I didn't mean to do that. It was an accident." You could then answer, "That's okay, no big deal."

If you are still confused or not sure, go find an adult. It is never okay for the first response to be to hit, push, or kick someone.

Celebrate Success and Learn New Lessons

The experiences your child has outside of the home are gauges for where they are emotionally and socially. As they get more confident in social situations, they may begin to need more help in the area of social nuances. This process will ebb and flow; sometimes you'll feel like your child is doing really well with experiences outside of the home, and at other times your child will seem to be struggling. Since inconsistencies are a hallmark of many sensory profiles, this should be an expected part of the process.

One of the last steps in this process is taking some time to review the out-of-home experience when you get home. First, you will take the opportunity to celebrate the successes with your sensory child. Next, you can have a quick mental review of what worked and what might need to be tweaked. Finally, for the situations that went all wrong, tap into the gift of clarity that these experiences provide.

Celebrate the Successes

This can be a crucial part of building your sensory child's self-esteem and confidence around their ability to navigate new or overwhelming situations. For some sensory kids, the immediate response is to go to the place of why it was bad, hard for them, or why no one liked them. If we have a system of reviewing all the successful pieces, we can help to change that pattern over time. Pick a quiet time after the event, such as bedtime or the next morning, to give them a quick review of the things they did well and had fun doing. Some examples of what you might highlight include:

- When you saw your child start a conversation or get a game going with other kids
- When your child came to ask you for a break or went off on his own to do something alone after a big group experience
- When your child came to ask for help when he was confused about a social exchange or a social nuance
- When he was laughing hard, playing a fun game, or genuinely just having fun

What Worked and What Needs Tweaking

This can be great to do with another adult who was with you at an event and can help you see the parts of the activity that went well for your child (and the parts that were a challenge) objectively. This will help you figure out how you can better prepare your child for future situations and how to support their social needs. Here are a few questions you can review after the situation:

- What pieces of the preparation before the event did your child seem to really connect with and refer back to in some way during the event?
- What were the times that your child seemed overwhelmed? What was he doing when he was the most socially connected and having the most fun?

- What were the signs your child was giving you that he needed a break? When he had a break, was he able to calm down and reconnect?
- Was there a new social nuance you noticed that was difficult for your child? Can you create a social tool or situation card to explain?
- Was your child able to pull away from the group when confused or feeling misunderstood, or did you need to remove him from the situation?

The Gifts of "All Wrong" Experiences

The awful experiences can be hard for kids and parents alike. However, they are, hands down, one of the most effective teaching tools we have. Let go of the judgment, guilt, or sadness over the situation and look underneath for the lessons you can get when everything goes "wrong." You often get extreme clarity about yourself, your child, and how you can best advocate for him.

I worked with one sensory girl who suddenly had a hard time socially, more than was typical for her. Mom described two party events where her daughter got physical with some neighborhood kids when overwhelmed socially, which was very unusual for her. Both of these situations were in front of close friends and family, so Mom was feeling awful for her child and overwhelmed about what might be causing this major shift in behavior. After looking at other things, Mom pinpointed a new medication that was recently added and that might have been having a negative impact on behavior. She called her child's doctor and after describing some of the new challenges and behaviors, the doctor immediately directed her to stop the medication. They later tried a different medication that ended up being a wonderful support for this child. Mom was able to look underneath all the emotion from those two "all wrong" experiences and get some very clear information about how to advocate for her sensory child.

Helping your child navigate new, overwhelming, or stressful situations outside of the home is going to be an ever-evolving process as your child grows and develops. The main focus should be helping your child have an understanding of what is easy for him in these experiences, what is hard, and tools to help learn a new skill and/or be successful. If our sensory kids can begin to learn the process of preparing themselves for a new situation, tapping into social tips and tools during the situation, taking a break when they need one, and patting themselves on the back for learning from the challenges, then they are already successful. These are the life tools that will serve them well as they navigate the sometimes unpredictable road ahead.

Chapter 11

Over the River and Through the Woods

Traveling with Your Sensory Child

Many of us spend the whole year looking forward to vacation time so we can travel to visit family, take a trip to a warm climate, or hit a tourist attraction or amusement park. We love the idea of stepping away from the day-to-day routine, enjoy seeing family and friends who live far away, and love the idea of visiting a new area. Unfortunately, these are all things that can be challenging for many sensory kids. Just as we need to prepare our sensory kids for these challenges individually, we need to have a plan in place for supporting them when traveling—a time when they are experiencing these all at once.

Many daily experiences have little pieces that might be challenging for our sensory kids. Going to a party with lots of new people, going on a day trip to a new place for a new experience, and going to see a movie for the first time can all be both challenging and successful outings for our sensory kids.

When we plan an out-of-town trip, we need to anticipate the things that are going to be initially hard for our sensory kids and come up with some ways to support the new places, new people, and new "home" that will be a part of the trip. In this chapter, we will discuss the Sensory Travel Plan, which includes understanding the new sensory vacation, tapping into sensory logistics when planning our trip, and how to prepare our sensory kids. These are all tools that will help our entire family make the most of the trip.

Sensory Travel Plan

The first step in embracing a trip with your sensory child is to have a conscious acceptance of the new definition of "vacation" for your family. It probably will not be fitting in as much as possible in a short time, extending your vacation by a day or two because the weather is great, surprising your family with a trip to Disney World, or staying with your Uncle Joe, who thinks all behavior challenges with kids come from a lack of discipline.

It might be helpful to have a few guidelines in mind for your family vacation that you review with your immediate family. By having a clear idea what your sensory vacation might look like, you will set clear expectations ahead of time, and you can always leave some room for adding in some extra activities if everything is running smoothly.

Highlights of the Sensory Vacation

- Not more than four–five days, at least initially.
- Visual aids and picture schedules, even on vacation.
- Lots of scheduled breaks and downtime.
- Parents splitting up on some parts of vacation to support their sensory child's experience and their typical child's experience.
- Some built-in visits to attractions that support a fascination.
- A little more TV time and/or computer game time than is normally allowed at home.
- Consider a regular vacation to the same rental house; this eliminates a big chunk of the preparation for you and the adjustment time for your sensory child.

Relax the Rules of Attendance

We all have this idea about vacations that "we are all going no matter what—this is our family time." Maybe we need to look at the fact that not everyone in our family needs to go on every vacation. Part of being a good parent is knowing what trips might be too much for your sensory child and might impact the experience for everyone else. You are not being a bad parent by not taking your sensory child on every trip! If you know your child can't handle amusement parks but a typical child loves them, you can do something that makes everyone happy. You could create an at-home vacation for your sensory child with one parent while another parent takes your typical child(ren) on a small trip to an amusement park.

Readjust What Is Doable

This is the biggest piece of setting up your family for a successful vacation. Come up with a game plan for what is doable in a day while on vacation. Look at some of the busiest days your child has in their schedule now and see what they look like. How many activities in the day? How many breaks are built in for your child, and how many times are they able to tap into a fascination? How are they at the end of this type of day? Overwhelmed? Weepy? Hyper? Knowing what your sensory child can handle in a day at home will give you a starting place for what they can handle in a day on vacation. Know that you will err on the side of fewer activities with the additional changes in the environment, people, and new "home" base.

Practice Makes Perfect!

Consider a dry run for a night or two locally before an upcoming longer trip. This may help you see what your sensory child loves about going on a trip, some of the things that are hard, things you wish you had with you, or things you wish you thought to do ahead of time. Nothing prepares you like really being in it!

Sensory Logistics

The secret to any successful trip is the planning that occurs ahead of time. With this in mind, here are some general guidelines:

Do What You Can for Yourself and Your Sensory Child Ahead of Time. Think about what you can do before you go that will make your travel time or vacation experience more enjoyable. If you are staying with family and traveling by plane, consider shipping a few things ahead of time or emailing a family member a list of a few things to have on hand that might make a big difference in your child's experience (for example, books on a favorite subject from a local library, or special/favorite foods to have in the house).

Location, Location, Location! Pick the best place to stay for your family. If you have family members who get easily overwhelmed with even the most polite, calm visitors, or family members who might have a lack of understanding of your sensory child's situation, consider staying in a hotel. You really will be setting everyone up for more quality interactions if you can follow your gut on this one without emotion.

Keep Consistencies Wherever You Can. Be conscious of building in some daily consistencies for your sensory child. Consider staying in the same hotel chain whenever you travel. Many hotels have great family suites with similar layouts in every location. If the suites come with a small kitchen, this can allow you to have one meal a day in the same place (not a loud restaurant). If your kids love swimming, find one that has a pool at every location; this alone can create some excitement. If you stay with family on a regular basis, consider staying with the same family members at the same home each visit. You can have a regular bedroom for your child, the same chill-out spot, and the same local attractions to visit—all things that will become routine and comfortable for them.

Create a Home Away from Home. This is one piece that can make overnight travel initially challenging. Our sensory kids will be in new experiences with new people all day and be coming "home" to an unfamiliar place at a time when they will need to regroup. You need to come up with a few ways to create a "home away from home." Think about what soothes and supports your sensory child at home and come up with ways to make travel versions of these supports.

- Create a Chill-out Zone on the road. Have a plan in mind at the hotel or the house you are staying in for a chill-out zone for your sensory child. This can be as simple as bringing some travel versions of favorite snugglies, blankets, books, and handheld sensory toys in a separate area so when they need a break, they know where to go.
- Relaxation at Bedtime. Try to create the same routine/systems that you do at home for on the road. Bring favorite music, a favorite book, and/or a favorite blanket. Tap into those things that work at home for bedtime as you will need a few of those tools while traveling.

Investigate the Lay of the Land. Before you go, spend some time learning about what is available to do around where you will be staying; parks, museums, movie theaters, arts and crafts places, and so on. This will help you be ready for action when you and your hosts need a break from each other, your typical child and your sensory child need a break from each other, or you need a plan for an unexpected open day with nothing scheduled.

Prepare, Prepare, Prepare!

As we know, the best thing you can do for your sensory child is to prepare them ahead of time for a new or overwhelming situation. This same idea is true for traveling, although in this situation, you will be preparing them for multiple changes over the course of multiple days!

Make a Family Trip Book

This is probably the most useful tool in supporting your sensory trip. With this one book, you will be able to accomplish many things. You will be able to give your sensory child a chronological map of experiences on the trip, pictures of people and places they may be seeing, and some information about the enticing parts of the trip so your child knows when he will be able to tap into a fascination. Here are a few ideas to help you make a sensory trip book:

Map It Out. Use the power of the internet and pictures you have on hand to help make a chronological map of the trip. This will allow you to use this as a preparation tool and as part of the daily schedule support. You could also include pictures of the house or hotel you are staying in. Include a map of where you will be going with routes highlighted and stopping points circled.

Have Time to Review. Get your Trip Book ready a week or two before leaving. You can read it daily with your sensory child, review a few times with the whole family, or leave it out for everyone to look at as needed. Having this visual support will prepare your sensory child for the changes that will be coming and give her an idea of what she might be seeing and doing.

Use Your Trip Book as a Travel Journal. Add blank pages in the Trip Book to fill out while on the trip. Use the Trip Book as a visual schedule support and as a journal of the trip. Your child can write something or draw a picture of their favorite thing of the day.

Build in Some Fascinations. Add some pieces to the Trip Book that you know will speak to your child. This is a way of creating continuity for them. No matter where you go, there are certain things that will make sense to them and be fun for them.

One family I worked with that was preparing for a sensory vacation had a child who loved numbers. Noticing and talking about numbers was a big part of his typical day. I encouraged Mom and Dad to include number spaces wherever they could in their Trip Book to help their child have a connection to all of the new things he would be encountering. They left a space to fill in the room number at the hotel, a space to write in the number of miles they were driving each day, and the number of times they got lost each day. Mom and Dad later told me that the number games were an active part of the trip and that they were able to incorporate a few additional number games with other vacation activities. (Everyone they went to visit on the trip was asked their favorite number, which was put on a separate page in the trip book next to their name!)

Remember the Good Times. After your trip, put the book in a safe place, as this will be a great tool to refer back to for the next trip. When your child reviews and remembers other successful trips, it will lessen the anxiety for the next trip. This will also help parents and caregivers remember strategies that worked as well as things that could be done differently for the next trip.

The Sensory Packing List

There is another easy, passive way to help your sensory child prepare for the trip: have them pack their own things. This is another opportunity for great executive function training, and it begins to paint a picture for your child about what awaits: dressy clothes they might have to wear, as well as important things they are bringing with them from home.

Here is an example of a packing list you might use. This could be laminated and used for each trip with a dry-erase marker to fill in the appropriate number of items. You could also just create your own version and print it out as needed for trips. For sensory children that need extra visual and processing support, you could use picture images in place of words on the packing list. For extra support, you could bring the packing list with you on the trip to help your child repack for the trip home. This can be a nice checklist to make sure your child has everything he brought with him.

My Packing List

Suitcase (clothes for trip)

_______ Pairs of Shorts
_______ T-shirts
_______ Long-sleeve Shirts
_______ Nice Outfits
_______ Pants
_______ Sweatshirts
_______ Jackets/Fleece
_______ Undies
_______ Socks
_______ Swimsuits
_______ Towels
_______ Toiletry Kit

Backpack (Chill-out Stuff)

_______ Favorite Books
_______ Electronics (DSi, iPod)
_______ Electronics chargers
_______ Cards, games, crafts
_______ Other _________________

Sleep Things
(Fall-asleep Stuff)

_______ Pillow
_______ Snugglies
_______ Pajamas/Nightgowns
_______ Robe and Slippers
_______ Sleeping Bag
_______ Bedtime Books
_______ Other _________________

Prepare Your Hosts

One of the most considerate things we can do when staying with friends or family is to give them some preparation for what living with your sensory child might be like. Helping your friends and extended family understand your child is not a onetime talk, but more of an ongoing conversation. As we know, the hallmark of many sensory profiles is inconsistency, so your friends and family may see many different facets of your child at different times. This, in itself, is hard for many people to understand. Since you want your friends and family to have the opportunity to connect with your child, give them the information they need to understand in bits and pieces. We want to slowly educate and foster a connection. We don't want to overwhelm anyone!

Keep It Simple. Think of the top two or three things that your host needs to know about your child to help the visit go as smoothly as possible, and don't forget to share all the great pieces about your sensory child! Focus on behavior, not diagnoses. My rule of thumb is to give family and friends a way to connect through the child's fascinations and interests, and an idea of main triggers or consistent challenges. For example, you might say, "Tommy needs about thirty minutes to get used to a new place, so he may just need to walk around by himself a bit, but once he is settled and playing, he loves anything to do with baseball and computers," or "Sarah has a hard time with small talk but loves marine life and would probably love to see the pictures and hear about your trip to the Caribbean."

Share Daily Routines. Inform friends or family you are visiting of the most important daily routines for your sensory child, so they can support them, instead of inadvertently disrupting them. For example, you might say, "Beth really does well when she knows what to expect, so maybe we could do a schedule every morning once we know what the plan is for the day."

Plan to Get Out of the House. Know that having any guests is a lot for many people to manage, so be sure to plan a few outings over the course of your visit. Give your hosts a break and go do something with your family occasionally. Leave your hosts at home to regroup and recharge. This can be a needed break for your sensory child also.

Planes, Trains, and Automobiles: Prepare to Get There

The last step in the process is preparing your child for how you will be traveling. Usually, car travel is one of the easiest ways to get there, since your child is probably already comfortable in that environment. Also, you can leave at the best time of day for your family, and you can control when and where you stop, how long between breaks, how often you can break, when you can eat, and so on.

If you are traveling far, air travel is often the only option. Yet an airport and airplanes contain many of the things that can overwhelm many sensory kids. Think about the airport: thousands of people rushing in fifteen different directions, bright lights and monitors everywhere, people bumping into you, music and intercom noise, and funny smells. This can leave kids overwhelmed and exhausted, and this is just day one of the trip! So, for sensory kids not used to or overwhelmed by air travel, a little extra preparation on this piece will be extremely helpful.

Prepare for Flying. Hit the library and grab some books on flying to help prepare your child for the trip. Also, check out online sites for videos of airports and security lines. It could be very helpful to investigate some of the accommodations that are available through the Transportation Security Administration (TSA). Security screening options and pre-boarding are a few of the accommodations available that might support travel with a sensory child. The TSA has a helpline for individuals with special needs called TSA Cares (1-855-787-2227) that travelers may call with questions about screening policies, procedures, and what to expect at the security checkpoint.

When our own little guy was quite young and on his first flying trip, he was, like many young sensory kids, pretty overwhelmed with the airport experience—and that was before we even got to security. Then all of a sudden, he was in a big line, taking his shoes off, and having to walk through a big "tunnel" with beeping noises without Mom or Dad. Once he got through (he was behind us because we thought that if he watched us, it would help!), he hit his point of being totally overwhelmed and ran back through the metal detector to get away from everything. That had everyone in security on edge, trying to talk to him, not letting me or my husband go back through to get him initially—just an all-around nightmare that had him on edge for the rest of the day!

If we had taken some time to prepare him for the airport and for airport security, things would have run more smoothly. We could have gone online to the TSA website and shown him how it works and what to expect, and then he would have had a visual map in his head about what was coming. This pre-travel preparation is especially important for sensory kids with AD/HD or ASD who can have challenges with observational learning—especially in new or stressful situations. After that experience and some additional preparation for the next travel day, he was much more accepting of the process. He knew the rules: he got his bin, put his stuff in the bin, pushed the bin ahead, and waited his turn to go through the tunnel. A much smoother travel day!

Anticipate the Hardest Pieces. What will be some of the hardest pieces for your sensory child? Will it be airport security, being on the plane, the big, loud airport, and what are some tools to have on hand. This is one of those situations we will tap into the Art of Distraction, the Power of Choice, and the Gift of the Fascination!

What to Have On Hand

Earplugs or noise-blocking headphones
Gum, lollipops, or gummies
Portable DVD and/or music with headphones
Small handheld sensory toys
Favorite books and games
Weighted lap blanket
Books about how airplanes work, about pilots, and so on.
Consider having a note from your doctor explaining your child's challenges

Making the Most of Your Trip

Usually, the hardest parts of the trip for your sensory child are going to be the night before you leave, when anxiety begins to kick in, the day of travel, and the first night you sleep in your "new" home.

- Be ready to encourage, support, distract, bring in fascinations, give choices, and use visual schedules.

- Be ready to pull out your portable sensory supports! Since you can't bring all your sensory toys with you, make do with bear hugs, crab walks, pillow fights, and piggyback rides.

By the second day, the new plan will start to sink in and look more familiar so things should be a bit calmer.

Pack That Schedule. We know that schedules and routines help at home, and this is also true when you are traveling and dealing with the unexpected many times during a day.

- Refer to the Trip Book as you are planning your day with your family.
- Bring a small whiteboard or make a blank laminated daily schedule outline that can be filled in daily with a dry-erase marker (see p. 184). Having a loose visual plan mapped for the day can help you tap into the Golden Tool on the road. This breaks it down and makes it manageable for everyone.
- Be ready to support inevitable changes in your schedule.

Resist the Urge to Overschedule. Be mindful of how your sensory child is managing each day and make adjustments as needed. Incorporate many breaks to let your child do calming activities that will help her regroup and reconnect. Focus here is on quality vacation experiences, not quantity.

Support for Mealtimes. Mealtime on the road—at restaurants and/or at friends and family members' homes—can be stressful, especially when happening three times a day. Consider making some periodic mealtime adjustments.

- Overall focus should be on quality experience, not quantity. It's much more important to have one or two successful meal experiences with family and/or friends than many experiences that are mediocre.

The Fun Things We Will Do Today on Our Family Trip

Breakfast!

1. ______________________________
2. ______________________________

Let's Take a Break!!

3. ______________________________
4. ______________________________

Lunchtime!

5. ______________________________
6. ______________________________

Let's Take a Break!!

7. ______________________________
8. ______________________________

Dinnertime!

9. ______________________________

Bedtime!

Remember:

1. At the end of the day, we will talk about our favorite things.
2. Let's have fun!

Copyright © 2009–2013 Systems for Sensory Kids, LLC. All rights reserved.

- Make time for immediate-family-only meals: maybe squeezing in some picnics outside if the weather permits, or a simple breakfast or lunch in the hotel suite would be a nice break.
- Build in some conversational entertainment to help your kid be part of the conversation and give friends and family an opportunity to get to know him. Some fun dinner games include: Dinner Games, Gather 'Round the Restaurant Game, Family Talk, Grandparent Talk, Teen Talk, and Buddy Talk (see Resource section for more info).
- Consider feeding kids first and popping in a kid movie when visiting friends and family. It is also important for you to feel like you are getting quality time to visit.

Bring in the Fascinations. With all that great research you did ahead of time, you should have some ideas for what's in the area that might tap into a fascination or special interest for your typical and sensory children. Getting your sensory child around something they intuitively get and understand can help ground them and prepare them for additional vacation time. You could also use the fascination breaks for your other children. Take them to do something that is special to them, as they may need some breaks from their sensory siblings while on a trip.

Trips and vacations can be such an important part of your family experience. They give you time to connect and share experiences in ways that are usually not possible during the week-in week-out routines at home. You can have these same opportunities when vacationing with your sensory kids. Taking some time to embrace the new sensory vacation, to plan ahead using sensory logistics, and to prepare your sensory child for the upcoming trip are all ways to get your vacation off on the right foot. Traveling together as a family can be an amazing confidence builder and create lasting memories of on the road successes!

Chapter 12

Love and Understanding

Empowering Those Who Teach and Care for Your Sensory Child

One of the most basic and necessary human needs is for love and respect from the important people in our lives. Our sensory kids do not want to be difficult, get into trouble, have a hard time staying on task, or have challenges making friends and fitting in. They want to be liked, they want to have friends, they want to be calm and connected, and, most important, they want to be understood.

Sensory kids will have plenty of peripheral interactions in their lives with people who do not understand them, and think they are just ill behaved due to poor parental discipline. Our main job as parents and advocates is to educate those who teach and care for our kids so that they too can embrace their strengths and help them be successful. This will be an ongoing process with family, friends, teachers, siblings, and babysitters. Taking some time to think about who your sensory child is—his strengths, his challenges, and how he connects with the world—will allow the people in their lives to love and understand them.

Start with Family and Friends

One of the most important steps is to let go of the idea that friends, family, and teachers will truly understand what you are going through as a parent of a sensory child. Unless they have a sensory child, they will never truly understand it all. However, you can help others understand and support your child.

Family can be one of the hardest groups to educate. They are the most emotionally connected to you and your sensory child, and this can lead to the denial of challenges or an inability to see the need for new rules for building a relationship with your sensory child. Let's talk about some simple ways we can educate and communicate information about your child to your friends and family.

Educating Your Spouse or Partner

Sometimes, in the early stages of learning that you are raising a sensory child, your spouse or partner may have a hard time seeing and accepting what you are seeing. Usually, the parental caregiver who is around the sensory child the most will be the first one to notice behaviors or reactions that are unusual. It may be how your child acts at play dates, birthday parties, daycare or school drop-off, and transitions to home that begin to give you important information. Sometimes your spouse or partner is not seeing these interactions. Here are a few things you can do to help your spouse or partner begin to see and understand what you are seeing in your sensory child.

- Have your partner witness the experiences where you are seeing the behaviors. After the event, talk about what you saw with your sensory child in relation to other children present.
- Talk to your pediatrician about what you are seeing. Having your pediatrician confirm your concerns may help your spouse or partner gain a better understanding.
- Find out about evaluations that are available to help you and your partner develop a broader understanding about appropriate development and where your sensory child may fit into the developmental spectrum.
- If your child is in daycare or school, get information about what the educators and caregivers are seeing. Having a solid understand-

ing of how your sensory child acts with other people may help him see it's not just you or your imagination.

Be patient and give your partner time. In the meantime, do what you need to do to support and educate yourself so that can best support and advocate for your child.

Extended Family and Friends

Keep it simple and relevant with family and friends. Give them quick, concrete information that will help them understand and interact with your sensory child. Make sure you are using everyday terms to describe your child to family and friends. It might feel natural for you to use diagnostic terms to describe your sensory child, but it's sometimes best to save those terms for the conversations you have with other sensory parents and clinicians (unless your family expresses a desire to learn more).

Having a solid idea of your sensory child's current strengths, fascinations, and challenges opens the door to building connections between family, friends, and your sensory child. It can be helpful to review the SSK Sensory Organizing Worksheet in chapter 4. There are a few questions that can be helpful to review when coming up with a quick plan on what you will communicate to family and friends:

- What are your child's strengths—things they are good at and love to do?
- List the three biggest challenges for your child that impact life and their experience with family and friends.
- What are common triggers for your child (things that get him/her upset, anxious, or overwhelmed)?
- How does your child calm down when upset?
- Does your child have a favorite color, character, or fascination?

The main rule is no overwhelming your friends and family with too much information at once. Look for simple ways to give family and friends a way to connect with your sensory child through fascinations and interests, and an idea of main triggers or consistent challenges.

As we did in chapter 11 when we were preparing our hosts, we might prepare our friends and family in a similar way—"Tommy needs about thirty minutes to get used to a new place, so he may just need to walk around by himself a bit, but once he is settled and playing, he loves anything to do with baseball and computers."

Other Parents

There may be other adults who will need more information, such as parents of your child's friends, coaches of teams, room parents at school, and others who spend time with your child occasionally. Again, you want to give just enough information at the start and then fill in as needed or when asked specific questions. The most important pieces here are:

- Acknowledging that you have a sensory child. This lets people know that we are not in denial and that we are able to discuss and educate if needed. This topic is always uncomfortable for parents to bring up or ask about, so by being open about certain sensory behaviors, you have opened the door.
- Letting these parents know that they can come to you if they have any questions or concerns. Unless we invite parents to come to us, they may feel uncomfortable and this may hurt our sensory child's social circle and may limit feedback we get about how our child is doing in different situations.

Take a gentle approach to educating and supporting family and friends as they begin to understand your sensory child, and accept that some families may not be receptive. Not too much at once, highlight the inherent strengths, and be open and available for questions and sharing information. This will be a big piece of building love and understanding for your sensory child.

Sibling Support

Now that we have some tools in place for supporting family and friends, let's spend some time supporting siblings. Life with a sensory child can be fun, unpredictable, explosive, loving, and everything in between. No one knows this better than typical siblings living with sensory kids. There are so many amazing things that our typical kids are learning from living with a sensory sibling: compassion, flexibility, and unconditional love. As great as that is, they are still managing some pieces that are hard, such as unpredictable behavior, challenges in social outings, sudden changes in plans that can be embarrassing and hard for siblings to understand, getting dragged along to many doctor and therapist appointments, and feeling the overall stress that this can bring to a family. Given the time it takes to support our sensory children, siblings can also get jealous of the "extra attention" they feel we give their sensory siblings or the rules they think are not applied equally.

As important as it is to support our sensory child, it is just as important to support and educate our typical kids on how to learn to live with a sensory brother or sister. Here are a few key ideas to keep in mind when teaching love and understanding to your typical children.

Gently Acknowledge What They Are Seeing

As we all know, kids are smart and have clarity that some of us lose over time. They see, hear, and put things together in their heads that some adults just miss. They might see explosive behavior, see that it is hard for their sensory sibling to sit through dinner, see a rough transition from school to home, and so on. We want our typical kids to learn to trust their intuition and instincts in all things, but especially in relation to what they are seeing with their sensory sibling. Begin to acknowledge in a simple way what they are seeing. A good way to start is to state in a matter-of-fact, nonjudgmental way what has happened. For example, "Samantha was just very angry about her homework. I think it is hard for her to turn off her play brain and turn on her work brain. Maybe some chill-out time will help."

Have a Name for Their Sensory Sibling's Profile

They are going to witness all that their sensory siblings do, and at some point they will figure out that their sibling has different challenges and reactions to certain things. Finding a name that accurately and appropriately describes their sensory sibling's profile is an important part of this process. Your sensory child's therapists or doctors can help you. There are a few key points to keep in mind as you work through this for your typical child(ren).

Consider their age and what they already know about their sensory sibling. It is not the time to pull out a big, scary word and leave them feeling more confused. Simple but honest is the goal. Tap into how they might describe their sensory sibling. You could even do a mini questionnaire to have them fill out about themselves, about a friend or two, and their sensory sibling (to camouflage what you are really doing). Some questions you might include are:

What are the three things you love to do?
What are three things that are hard for you?
What is your favorite food?
What is your favorite game/toy?
What is your favorite TV show?

This allows you to hear some of the words they might use to describe their sensory sibling and maybe a name can come from one of those. With this questionnaire, you are also allowing your typical child to see the whole sibling and not just the difficult pieces.

Make Sure You Get Time Alone with Your Typical Kids

Our sensory kids can demand more of our time, demand more of our attention, and need more support during different cycles or times of the year. This means that our typical kids will have periods of feeling less important, that their sensory sibling always comes first, and that they get all the extra help. These are valid feelings and in order to counterbalance them, both caregivers need to get some regular time alone with our typical kids. It can be a weekly date for lunch, a walk, errands you always do together, library or playground visit, or even time alone at home. Almost anything will work here as long as you are one-on-one with no sensory siblings around to interrupt or distract.

This time can be a critical part of developing an open, honest relationship with your typical child and can be a big piece in helping them feel supported.

Get Typical Kids Their Own Support

The last piece to be aware of when supporting our typical kids is to know that they may get to a place of needing their own support for navigating life with a sensory sibling. Living with an unpredictable sibling can leave some typical siblings feeling anxiety, anger, or sadness. As parents, we are sometimes too close to this and unable to help our typical kids objectively. The power in sibling support can come from seeing and learning from other typical siblings, knowing that "I am not alone in this," as well as relationships with professionals. Though there are some very specific sibling programs available in some areas, most parents seem to have the best luck finding individual therapy or more general group therapy to support their typical kids. (See the Resource section.) Knowing that people are out there to help when you need it can be a wonderful lesson for all kids and is especially true for some kids living with a sensory sibling.

You Are Parenting Different Kids with Different Rules

One of the harder pieces for our typical kids to understand is that parenting different kids means different rules. We may have different behavior and chore expectations as well as different consequences in place for our typical kids compared to our sensory child. Because our sensory kids can have a low threshold for frustration, have a hard time staying on task, and have challenges with gross and fine motor skills, some of the chores we might ask our typical kids to do will be different or structured in a different way than the ones we ask our sensory child to do.

One way to make this piece somewhat consistent is to have a similar visual plan in place for all kids to know what is expected (like the Central Message Area in chapter 8). The amount of time all the kids are doing chores can be the same, but maybe the tasks are slightly different and perhaps your sensory child gets some extra visual support (like the Chore Card). You could also have a similar reward plan for each child, such as a certain number of completed tasks or chores gets you a certain reward.

I worked with one mom whose sensory daughter, Sarah, had anxiety disorder and OCD and had a very hard time with certain chores. There were certain things that she was asked to do that would result in a meltdown due to her hyperfocus on getting the chore done perfectly. For example, asking her to make her bed was a chore that never ended well because Sarah would spend an inordinate amount of time trying to make the bed look "perfect" and would end the chore in tears because she believed that she never could. So, although the making your bed chore was expected of Sarah's typical siblings, we created different chores for Sarah that allowed her to be more successful. The chores Sarah were given had a certain structure to them that were logical and comforting, like putting certain toys in labeled bins, organizing her arts and craft supplies in a labeled, plastic drawer system, and putting her clothes away. Mom made chore time consistent by having a labeled chore area with a checklist for each child and certain times of the week when chores were done.

In the Classroom: Helping Teachers Support Your Sensory Child

Once you have some plans in place for love and understanding for your family and friends, you can start spending some time with the other important people in your sensory child's life, like their teacher. Helping teachers understand and support your child is such an important piece of making the school experience positive. Teachers have many kids they are supporting, with as many as 10 percent of each class needing some accommodations in place. That's a lot for anyone to manage! Your job is to make supporting your child easier for his teacher.

We are going to take our Golden Tool and apply it to helping our teachers:

1. Break down your child's needs.
2. Help your child's teacher focus on the top two or three challenges.
3. Be available to make visual aids to support challenges and follow through at home.

A few guidelines when working with teachers:

Ease Into It

Do not go right in to the teacher with evaluations and diagnostic reports right off the bat. Give the teacher some time to get to know your child in an unbiased way. Most teachers can spot sensory kids right away, and it is important to let them come up with their own list of strengths and challenges. Many times, our sensory kids will perform better at school than they do at home.

Paint a Simple Picture of Your Child

When it is time to discuss your child, give a quick snapshot of your child: focus on strengths, behaviors, challenges (instead of possible diagnoses), and academic and social goals for the year. To help your child's teacher, you should also share one core strategy that you know has worked. For example, if you know your sensory child is prone to avoidance techniques when it's time to do an undesired activity, you could help your teacher create some structure around this challenge. Say your child is asking to use the bathroom every time she has to transition into a challenging task or activity. You could suggest her teacher use a bathroom ticket system (certain number of bathroom tickets allotted per day). This sets clear expectations and is a great visual aid, but still allows your sensory child to have some control over using this as a coping mechanism. This is a great way to help your child's teacher build a tool kit one step at a time.

Be Available But Not Annoying

With the number of sensory kids climbing every year and school budgets getting smaller and smaller, many sensory kids and their teachers may be working without much additional support. Most teachers will be happy for some extra help with supporting children for success in the classroom, so make yourself available but don't overdo it or hound your child's teacher. Come up with a system for periodically checking in. Take special notice of when your child is more rigid, anxious, or distracted at home, as that usually translates to school. These are times teachers may need help with support and strategies. For example, say the teacher mentions that your child is having a hard time understanding and playing along with the rules during outside games at recess time. You could create a visual aid, like a Situation Card (see chapter 10), that explains why there are rules in games, why it's expected that you will follow the rules, and what might happen if rules aren't followed. This is a simple but powerful way to help your child and your child's teacher.

Build In Consistencies Between Home and School

This will help teachers more than you know! When you pick two or three important strategies to reinforce at home, you are setting your child up to be more successful with them at school (thus helping his teachers!). Consistency will help both of you. Examples would be same wording and images for schedules, consistent color coding for subjects, or the same outline format for any writing project.

Make Homework Manageable

Homework can be a real struggle for many sensory kids. They have been working hard all day to be as connected, attentive, and calm as possible, and they often come home with little reserve left for homework. Work with your child's teacher to create an understanding of homework expectations. You might need to find the middle ground between completing every homework assignment and ensuring that your sensory child understands the main concepts (review back to the academic goals for the year). Maybe your child doesn't need to do word searches or crossword puzzles (time consuming and not a bang for the homework buck), but reading, spelling words, and writing assignments are a must do.

Executive Function and Time Management Training All Day, Every Day

Executive function and time management training will be some of the best long-term supports you can give your child's teachers (and some of the best life skills for your child!). Many teachers will be working under the assumption that most kids are working at the same level when it comes to planning and organizing. We know that many sensory kids struggle with this, and that is when homework gets lost, deadlines get missed, and books get forgotten, all things that add time and frustration to a teacher's day. Every school task, project, and homework assignment done at home should have the same visual supports, written plans, weekly calendar maps, and checklists.

Understand the Natural Arc of the School Year

Be aware of the natural ebb and flow of the school year. Know what times of year are typically hard for your sensory child because of new routines, more or different transitions, pressure from testing, or a heavier academic work load. Planning for these cycles on a monthly basis supports both your child and his teacher. For example, you might break the school year into three sections: September through December, January through March, and April through June.

Section 1: September through December

September: Supporting the New School Routine. Focus on helping your child learn the new schedule and routine at school. Have at home a copy of the daily schedule and new morning routine in the classroom for your child to review at night or on the ride to school.

October: Paperwork Management. This month you might focus on solidifying the paperwork management systems: how to get the right books and papers home and back to school. Work with your child's teacher on classroom strategies already in place to help this process. Color-coding systems, locker organization, and backpack maintenance routines can create that structure to help your child manage. Pay attention to where the consistent challenges are, and work with your child and his teacher to refine a better system or routine as needed for problem areas.

November: Homework Strategies. Since mid- to late fall typically brings an increased academic schedule—the introduction of the year's curriculum and increasing homework demands—this is the time to focus on study and homework strategies. Have a designated homework place that is quiet and has everything your child might need. Have a blank laminated homework and break plan schedule to help your child map out his time. For extra support, graphic organizers can be a great way to help get your child started on challenging homework. You can also laminate and keep in the homework area for easy access a few step-by-step planners for organizing and writing a story, memorizing tips and tricks, and note-taking techniques.

December: Holiday Survival Mode. Holiday time can be overwhelming for sensory kids, with the additional stimuli, different schedules, extra free time, and holiday parties. Holidays are generally a stressful time for all of us, and our sensory kids can be influenced by the anxiety levels around them. Try your best to maintain a sense of normalcy in schedules and routines. To support all the changes to the normal routines at school and at home, having a more detailed daily or weekly calendar can be a great support for this month.

Section 2: January through March

January: Remembering the Routine. After the holidays, this month is about getting back into the academic routine. This is a great time to reinforce systems and routines you put in place over the fall as your child moves into another time of core academic learning. This can be a good time to use that inside active zone to give your sensory child a physical release during those darker winter days (if you're in such a climate!) when outside play is less likely.

February: Time Management. Mid- to late winter can be another time of intense academic learning. Creating some time management systems can be an important piece of supporting these times. Hang a whiteboard weekly calendar for homework/study planning. For bigger projects, put in end dates and work backward to create smaller deadlines. This will help your child see the smaller chunks and not just the big, overwhelming end date. Check in weekly to see if they need help adjusting plans to ensure they are staying on target.

March: Plugging Along. This can be another reinforcement time: a long month with frustration or boredom starting to build. Kids have been plugging along all winter and are starting to get tired of school and schoolwork. The key here is keeping it fun and exciting! Tweaking an existing system in a fun or colorful way or tapping into multisensory ways of learning (use websites, flip cameras to make a video, fields trips on weekends to support what they are learning in school) are a few ways you can jazz it up this month.

Section 3: April through June

April: A Second Wind. This month can give everyone a new bounce of energy: changing weather, longer and brighter days can help sensory kids feel reenergized. Getting them outside and doing an activity or sport that gets them a physical release can be a great support for learning and focusing at school.

May: Almost There. May can be the culmination of many extra activities at school like music concerts, plays, and athletic events. Though these are exciting, they can be overwhelming for many sensory kids. If helpful, create a few Situation Cards for these experiences. (See chapter 10.)

June: Checking Out. This can be a long month for teachers and students, so keeping your sensory child engaged and on-task can be a challenge. Mapping out this month can be a big help. Highlight any field trips or field days at school, creating a "countdown to summer" game, adding a "summer frozen treat" night, and beginning to talk up any early summer activities like camps or classes can help your sensory child manage the excitement level this month. After school is done for the year, have a plan ready to map out the unstructured time for the summer. (See chapter 9.)

Working to support your child's teacher is such an important piece of their success at school. Our teachers are working very hard, sometimes with limited support for special needs in the classroom. Most teachers will be very appreciative of parents who understand their child's way of learning, are proactive in creating supports for challenging times, and are available to help teachers help their child.

Preparing the Babysitter

Other people you need to consider supporting and educating are babysitters and caregivers that work with your family. We know that getting time away from our kids is important to our individual health, to our marital relationship, and sometimes necessary for our employment. For someone who is new to your family, spending some time helping her understand your family, schedules, routines, and special information about your sensory child will help her do her job well.

Timing Is Everything

Pick the right time to go out. If possible, pick the times that are the calmest, easiest part of your child's day. For example, if your child does well when the day is winding down and is more relaxed at dinner and bedtime, that could be a good time for you to be out. If your child has a tough transition to bed, you may want to plan afternoon outings until your child and your babysitter seem more comfortable with each other.

Same Time, Same Place

Consider having a regular night out, such as every Tuesday night or every other Saturday night. Since you know how well schedules and routines work in preparing your child for what is coming, if they know that every Tuesday is your night out, they will be prepared and, most likely, ready.

Arrange for a Pre-Visit

Have any new sitters or caregivers come over for a thirty-minute pre-visit. This will give your sitter and your children a chance to get to know each other in a calm and relaxed way. For extra support, you could take a picture of the babysitter and hang it up in your central message area.

Top 5 Simple Tips Sheet

Create a simple map for your babysitter, called a Top 5 Simple Tips Sheet, to relay valuable information about your child and create a plan for your child to follow.

As you start the Top 5 Simple Tips Sheet, review key points from the SSK Sensory Organizing Worksheet from chapter 4, specifically questions number 2 and number 3.

1. Make a simple schedule. This will help your babysitter and your sensory child know what to expect while you are out.
2. Highlight the things your sensory child and typical child love to do and the things that instantly calm and connect them.
3. Highlight the common triggers or challenges your sensory child might experience.
4. Plan something special. Have something exciting on tap: a TV show or movie that the kids have been dying to see, a special dessert, a special game that is only done with the babysitter, or a later bedtime are all easy ways to build some excitement and some "support" from the kids.
5. Review the bedtime plan. Have a simple but clear bedtime routine mapped out, since this transition can be harder for sensory kids when out of the usual routine (different time, different people). Creating a bedtime plan visual aid and helping your caregiver add her own bedtime tradition can be a great support (like reading a certain book or telling the same bedtime story).

The Babysitting Plan

You might print out and laminate the schedule, which would allow you to fill one out for each babysitting situation. Like other visual aids, you can use words, images, drawings—whatever works best in communicating to your sensory child!

Babysitting Plan

Plan for the Night

What we LOVE to Do:

What makes us Crabby:

Special Treat for the Night:

Bedtime Plan:

Copyright © 2009–2013 Systems for Sensory Kids, LLC. All Rights Reserved.

Tips for You!!

Limit the Check-ins. It is best to limit how often you are checking in right off the bat. You don't want to make it easy for your child to know when you might be calling or how to get anyone to call you.

Don't Let Behavior Dissuade You. If your child is having a hard time, plan to go out anyway. Frequently, a changing of the guard can be enough to help your child shift into a calmer place, and they will learn an important lesson—that their behavior will not change your plans. Also, sensory kids often save the most challenging behavior for those closest to them, so you might begin to see that their behavior is worse for you before or after you go out but it is fine for the babysitter.

Be Clear About When a Sitter Should Call You. You need to let your sitter know when they should call you. Some examples of when your sitter should call: if your child is not shifting out of challenging behavior and this is impacting your typical kids (they are feeling scared or sad), your sitter is uncomfortable, or if your child ever talks about hurting themselves or someone else. You may have some of your own ideas of what warrants a phone call—just be sure to be clear with your babysitter or caregiver. You also may need to create a set rule that only the babysitter can talk to parents on the phone while they are out to avoid a possible power struggle and limit triggers for inappropriate behavior.

Have Important Numbers and Medical Info Handy. Have important phone numbers (your contact info, doctors' numbers, house address) and all medication and supplement information (dosages, times of day taken), and health insurance information all stored in a clearly marked area.

It is so important to get some time away from your parenting role. Finding a good babysitter or caregiver can be such a gift. Take the extra steps of making sure she gets to know your family and understands what works for all of your kids, with some extra attention given to plans and strategies that work for your sensory child. Being clear and honest about your child's needs and possible challenges, as well as strategies and plans about handling tougher times, will help your babysitter feel supported, which may translate into a long-term relationship with your family.

Now we have some great strategies in place to help our sensory child feel love and understanding from all of the important people in his life every day. This will have a huge impact on our child's confidence and success. The last step on our Sensory Organizing journey is aimed at organizing you to get the right support team in place for you, your sensory child, and your family.

Chapter 13

Becoming an Advocate

Getting the Support for Success

While *The Sensory Child Gets Organized* can offer you strategies and systems for supporting your sensory child at home, it does not replace critical medical, clinical, and educational support. Now that we have spent some time talking about how to support your sensory child in the home and in the world, we need to talk about ways you can build the right support team for you, your family, and your sensory child as you all navigate the ever-changing life experiences at home and at school.

As I mentioned at the beginning of this book, one of the best gifts we can give our entire family during this process is the ability to meet ups and downs inherent to this journey. Some of the tools come from the structure, routines, and visual aids we have already discussed and some of the tools will come from various forms of professional support.

The statistics of mental illness in America suggest that many children, teenagers, and adults will need a level of professional help at some point during their lives. The National Alliance on Mental Illness states that one in four adults—approximately 57.7 million Americans—experience a mental health disorder in a given year, and about one in ten children live with a serious mental or emotional disorder. On the bright side, it is well documented that if you can get the right treatment for your child, it works to support many pediatric mental health issues.

When you are honest about current needs within your family, as well as open to considering available supports and treatments, your family members will learn to recognize when they need help. They will also begin to learn what tools help them get through these situations in a calmer and more confident way. Seeing the ebb and flow of periodic needs in a sensory family will give everyone awareness of when it is time to ask for help and get a plan of support in place.

Like many other things you have embarked on during this sensory journey, there are a few key things to understand as you begin this process of building a support team.

- You should work to establish a long-term support system. It is critical that you find people who understand and appreciate your philosophy of parenting your sensory child. To avoid exposing your child or other family members to professionals who may not be the right long-term fit, set up initial appointments just for you and the potential professional. If, after the first appointment, you do not feel like this person is the right fit for your sensory child or your family (and you are not in a crisis situation), keep looking.
- Once you have the right people in place, be open to learning new techniques and trying new ideas that have some peer-reviewed evidence supporting their use for children with your child's sensory profile.
- Other typical members of your family may need periods of support as well, especially during those cycles of intense challenging behavior at home. Giving other family members long-term coping tools is an amazing gift.
- The types of support and number of people you work with will constantly change based on current needs. Have the core team on hand so that when needs shift, you will have a comfortable, familiar person ready to work with your sensory child.
- Be ready for trial and error. Don't get discouraged if the first therapy strategy doesn't work. It may take some time to find the right strategies and techniques that work for your sensory child and your family.

- As we did when we began our journey into Sensory Organizing, we need to also work on getting ourselves into a supported, coachable place. So the last key point will lead us into our next section: creating supports for you!
- Get help for yourself! As they say, you are incapable of helping anyone else until you help yourself, and this is very true when supporting a sensory child at home. It will make you calmer, more connected, and less reactive—all things that will make you a better parent.

Supports for You

The most important place to start when building a professional support team for your sensory child is to build one for yourself, the primary caregiver. As the parent of a sensory child, you will be navigating professional support, medical needs, accommodations at school, social skills training, and likely a good deal of emotional stress in addition to all the other "normal" things that come along with raising a family. In order to manage successfully, you need to do a few things to keep your own mental health balanced and supported.

Redefine "Organized"

Create your own definition of what organized means for you right now. If you are the parent of a sensory child, your definition of organized is not going to mean a simplified linen closet or a neatly labeled pantry. Focus your organizing on things that will impact your needs today like educational and/or medical paperwork systems, homework supports, simple meal planning, and maintaining an effective Central Message Area. This one shift will be life-changing!

Focus on the Quality of the Experience, Not Quantity

Think in terms of value added for everything you add to your family schedule and make sure you have some downtime as a family. Be selective in after-school activities and make sure they are quality experiences for your children. For your children, pick activities that are a good physical release, that support one of their fascinations, tap into a creative outlet, or provide a great social learning opportunity. This goes for family meals also. It's much better to have two to three quality family dinners each week than five or six that are rushed and not relaxing. This will be good for you, your sensory child, and the whole family!

Have Your Own Escape and Regulate Spot

When you are going to be asking your sensory child to go to her escape and regulate spot when she needs a break, you had better have one for yourself! This is some of the best kind of modeling we can do for our children. When you feel yourself getting overwhelmed, go sit in your chill zone and get reconnected to the present moment.

Therapy for You

If you are stuck in any way in a place of guilt, anger, sadness, or depression about raising a sensory child, work with a professional to handle your feelings. Though all of these feelings are normal, when they are stuck in a negative pattern, they will limit your ability to advocate for and effectively support your sensory child.

Support Groups

There are many wonderful support groups out there for all types of sensory diagnoses and experiences you might be dealing with (please see Resources in the back of this book.). Many groups provide genuine and authentic support and creative ways to share parenting or caregiver information. There is also something comforting in feeling that you are not alone and being around others who understand what you are going through. But, as with any service or professional, make sure any group you join matches your outlook and philosophy.

Parenting and Professional Conferences

There are also wonderful parenting and professional conferences available online or in person. These can give you very practical information on the profile you are supporting at home. Make sure you pick conferences that are geared toward practical understanding of and strategies for the sensory profile you are supporting, not geared toward explanations of intricate research aimed at professionals. Leaving a conference completely overwhelmed will do nothing to support your day-to-day understanding of your child. Conferences also allow you to connect with other parents who are supporting the same profiles, and these relationships can be a wonderful part of creating your own support group.

Periodically Break Away

This is critical! Have a few things you do that are not related to parenting or special needs in any shape or form! While there will always be a part of you that will be permanently connected to your experience as the parent of a sensory child, it can be so therapeutic to reconnect with a few things you used to love to do before family and kids came along. Yoga, art classes, exercise, or getting together with friends (and not talking about your child's issues) will enhance your ability to parent and support your sensory kids. It is okay and healthy to compartmentalize pieces of your life: be a part of a group that knows you for you.

You Can't Do It Alone: Developing a Sensory Support Team

Once you have done some work on supporting yourself, you can work on getting the correct supports in place for your sensory child, and your whole family. This can mean ongoing professional support or periodic periods of professional support when your sensory child or your family seems to be in a new challenging place. Having the right team can be instrumental in long-term growth for your family.

This will often be a process unto itself. Be an advocate for yourself and your child, talk to other parents, learn about the specific focus of different clinicians. You might need to work hard to find people who really connect with you and your sensory child. These people need to be your security blanket, people you can really trust. There will be ups and downs raising a sensory child, and I can tell you from personal experience how powerful it is to have someone who can help "me" as a parent, as well as my child during those inevitable difficult periods.

As you begin to explore the different resources and supports that might be available for your sensory child, it is important to note that, even though some services are mandated by federal law, the professional and educational services available can vary widely from state to state, county to county, and even school district to school district. Many states have resources to help you understand the guidelines for your area. As you begin to develop a support team, some of the professionals may include your pediatrician, early intervention staff, speech therapist, occupational therapist, cognitive-behavioral therapist, behavioral analyst, developmental pediatricians, neuropsychologists, psychologists, and therapists. For most families, your team might ebb and flow between two to four people depending on where your child is developmentally and what they are experiencing currently. Now I want to take some time to highlight the possible roles of some of the different professional supports available to us to help us on our journey.

Pediatrician

The pediatrician is the most important ground-level guide for your child's development. He or she will be the objective eye who begins to know your child from day one, and very often your pediatrician is the person who begins to notice or concur with you that developmental milestones are not being met or that your child's behavior is worrisome. This is where the journaling we talked about in chapter 3 comes in handy. Having detailed notes and observations of behavior, unusual habits, and sensory challenges will be extremely helpful to your pediatrician who is only seeing your child periodically.

Your pediatrician can be the most important person in helping you to get the critical early support for your child. He or she will often be the person who refers young children to developmental pediatricians, child development centers, and Early Intervention for evaluation and treatment. If you have a pediatrician who is not feeling the same concern that you are feeling, ask for a second opinion. Meet with another pediatrician in the group or ask for a referral to a developmental pediatrician—a pediatrician who specializes in developmental, behavioral, and learning issues in infants, children, and teenagers. Don't be afraid to challenge your doctor, respectfully but forcefully, if something really doesn't feel right to you. In my experience, few parents are looking to find a developmental issue with their child, so if a parent is seeing something, it is usually worth investigating.

Early Intervention

Early Intervention can be the first line of defense for parents when looking to get early treatment or therapy to help support their child's developmental or medical challenges. As stated in *A Parent's Guide to Special Education,* by Linda Wilmshurst and Alan W. Brue, the Individuals with Disabilities Educational Act requires that each local education authority (typically, your school district) identify, evaluate, and provide special education and related services to meet the needs of children under three who would be at risk for being developmentally delayed if early intervention services were not provided. In some states, the services are provided by the department of education while in others the services are provided by the health department. Again, the challenge here is that the Early Intervention eligibility requirements can vary significantly from state to state, meaning that a child with an autism spectrum disorder (ASD) in one state could get broader support than an ASD child in another state.

In *The Sensory Processing Disorder Answer Book,* occupational therapist Tara Delaney discusses early options for your child with developmental challenges. If your child is under three, your pediatrician should be able to refer you to your local Early Intervention (EI) Program. EI provides a free multidisciplinary evaluation for your child and, based on the results of the testing, services for your child are covered through EI or through your family's health insurance, depending on the state. EI will also provide support for medical challenges, like vision and hearing, as well as support for developmental challenges with speech, physical, and occupational therapy. Among the concerns that might prompt parents to seek EI are speech or hearing challenges, sensory challenges (overwhelmed with sensory input or needs heavy sensory input), fine or gross motor delays, repetitive behaviors, or not meeting certain developmental milestones.

Once an evaluation is complete and needs are identified, services are assigned. Some of the services EI will provide include speech therapy, occupational therapy, physical therapy, special education, and applied behavior analysis, among others.

Speech and Language Therapy

Speech and language therapy supports the development of communication (receptive language and expressive language), articulation (difficulty in pronunciation), as well as oral motor function (such as swallowing and eating). Speech and language challenges can be a standalone issue or can coexist with many other sensory diagnoses we have discussed in this book. Through EI, this service can be done at your house but after the age of three, if the child continues to need speech and language therapy, most often the services would be handled either at home or at your child's regular or special ed pre-school.

Some common speech challenges parents might see early on include a child who is not speaking to express wants and needs, who has a limited vocabulary, who is not engaging in reciprocal conversation, who does not follow simple directions or understand what is being said, a child who echoes or copies what is being said to him/her, or a child who has a hard time saying certain sounds and words consistently.

Occupational Therapy

In *The Out-of-Sync Child,* Carol Stock Kranowitz defines an occupational therapist as someone who helps children with motor and behavior challenges to learn skills to support their personal, social, and academic development. When treating sensory challenges, the main idea is to provide the correct amount of sensory support: just enough to challenge and develop the sensory system, but not too much to make the child shut down or become overloaded. What is calming to one child might be overwhelming to another child. Occupational therapists are instrumental in helping you learn your child's specific sensory needs and come up with ways to build sensory supports into your child's day.

Some things a parent might see early on that might suggest needs in this area include a child who consistently crashes into things or seems to move nonstop, a child who always seems overwhelmed with loud noises, tags on clothes or seams on socks, or changes to routines, a child who appears "floppy" or has low muscle tone, or a child who seems clumsy or awkward when using gross or fine motor skills. Again, OT needs may be a standalone issue or may be a piece of another diagnosis that doesn't fully emerge until a child is older.

Cognitive Behavioral Therapy

In their book *Therapy 101,* Jeffrey C. Wood and Minnie Wood describe cognitive behavioral therapy (CBT) as a treatment that looks at the ways your thoughts, behaviors, and emotions influence each other and your overall mental health. CBT can begin to teach you how to change your automatic thoughts and come up with new plans to help you modify or change your behavior. CBT can be an extremely effective treatment for all types of sensory kids because it is a very tangible process that uses concrete visual aids and strategies to help a child shift into a new way of thinking. CBT is particularly good for sensory kids diagnosed with AD/HD, mood disorders, depression, anxiety, OCD, and Asperger's. There is rarely the option of getting CBT through EI or through school districts under an IEP, so this is something most families have to arrange for privately.

Applied Behavior Analysis

Applied behavior analysis (ABA) is based on the idea that your actions are learned from your environment through imitation of those around you, as well as the provision of tangible rewards for certain behaviors. The goal of ABA is to change observable behaviors instead of changing your internal thoughts. The idea is that if one behavior is reinforced and another is not, you will learn to do the behavior with the reinforcement attached to it. For example, the sensory child who is learning how to grow and develop social skills may work with an ABA therapist and a reinforcement system around targeted social behaviors (like eye contact when saying hello) until those skills are learned. ABA also works well for many sensory kids like those diagnosed with AD/HD, autism, and/or developmental delays, and can be one of the supports used for treating OCD.

Pediatric Psychiatrists

Pediatric psychiatrists are medical doctors who work with children who have mental health issues as well as organic, physical brain problems. They are also the primary sources for medications you might use to address the behaviors seen in many sensory diagnoses. Most professionals agree that, many times, the best treatment for many types of sensory profiles is a combination of medication and long-term therapy like cognitive behavioral therapy or applied behavior analysis.

Pediatric Neurologist

According to the American Academy of Pediatrics, a pediatric neurologist deals with problems involving the nervous system such as seizures, head injuries, muscle weakness, developmental disorders, and behavioral disorders.

Pediatric Neuropsychologists

According to the American Psychological Association, a neuropsychologist studies the relationship between brain function and behavior and how various neurodevelopmental disorders, diseases, and injuries of the brain affect emotion, perception, and behavior. When working with children, they use standardized testing protocols that help them look at cognitive function skills such as attention and executive function, language, motor skills, memory and learning, processing speed, and social perception. With the results of these tests, a neuropsychologist can initiate or confirm a diagnosis. While they cannot prescribe medications or see clients for long-term therapy, neuropsychologists can play a critical role. They help you identify the core challenges and make a diagnosis for your child, and they outline a game plan for support, which could include: implementing the right medicinal support, getting the right therapies in place, and giving you and your child's teachers excellent strategies for supporting their way of learning. Although not provided through school districts, some parents may find it helpful to have updated neuropsychological evaluations around main academic transitions—elementary to middle school and middle school to high school—to revisit core challenges and learn new strategies to support their long-term success.

Developing the right team for your family and your sensory child is such an important piece of long-term success in managing your child's needs, helping them understand who they are and what works for them, and that, like all of us, they are going to need some help along the way.

Creating Systems for Sensory Support

Once you have your professional team in place, you will begin to see that there is a lot of information to manage. It can make you feel so frustrated and overwhelmed when you know your child already had a procedure, an evaluation done, or tried a medicine unsuccessfully, but you can't find the paperwork to support your claim. Bottom line: when you can access the information you need, when you need it, you are better able to advocate for your child. In this section, we are going to spend some time creating some systems to help you manage all the information coming your way.

Paperwork

Most families immediately see the first thing they are going to have to manage—paperwork! As a professional organizer, I know that paperwork management is something that almost every family struggles with, but paperwork exists at a whole new level when you are supporting anyone with a medical need. Creating paperwork systems will help you access what you need, make sure you are getting paid/reimbursed appropriately by your insurance company, help you keep your child safe with medications/supplements, and help you tap into therapy strategies more efficiently.

Paperwork Systems

For most families, three binders will work the best when managing all the sensory paperwork: Medical Binder, Therapy Binder, and Education Binder. We will talk about the first two binders here and talk about the Education Binder in the next section on advocating for your child at school.

A few things to remember as you get started:

- Even if you have a big pile of paperwork to sort and get organized, this is one of those things we always make bigger in our heads than it is in reality. Just sit down and get started!
- Create a staging area where you have labeled sheets on the ground that help you begin to categorize your paperwork into appropriate groups.
- Start with good materials: a big, solid binder, strong tab sections with big, clear labels, and clear page protector inserts, which are good for keeping important paperwork (especially original documents) protected but easy to see.
- Arrange all sections of each binder in chronological order with the most recent on the top. If the binder gets too full, take out the back, oldest part of a section, put it into a labeled, sealed envelope and store in a plastic file box or bin labeled "Medical Archive," with the date range of what's stored. Make sure it is stored in a dry area to best assure the long-term life of paperwork.
- Since many doctors and insurance companies are going paperless and information is being filled out and completed online, you can create a virtual filing system on your computer identical to your paper filing system. This means that you will have both a hard copy and an electronic system for managing your sensory paperwork—essential in the unhappy event of a power outage or natural disaster.

The Medical Binder

This binder will hold all things regarding your sensory child's physical health and all the billing and reimbursement submissions with your health insurance company. Here are some of the things you might have in this binder:

- Pediatrician Paperwork: A copy of your child's medical record, updated information on all vaccinations, vaccination titers, flu shots, allergies to medications, etc.
- Blood Work: Copies of any blood work or other lab results for your child.
- Other Medical Info: If you have worked with an allergist, a naturopath, an infectious disease expert, each should have his or her own section in this binder.
- Medications and Supplements: This is a very important section for the health and safety of your child. This section would include information about any medications or supplements your child has been on in the past along with information on results when taken (see Medication Checklist Form below). In the front of this section, have a list of all medications and supplements your child is currently taking, with dosages, schedules, and prescriber contact information. Also, in the case of medication, include a copy of the pharmacy fact sheet on the medication that includes the name of medication, directions on how to take it, side effects, precautions, and drug interactions. Make sure anyone who takes care of your child knows where this information is located.
- Health Insurance Section: This section will hold all copies of reimbursement requests for all services related to your child. Some families find it helpful to keep the medical reimbursement requests here and the therapy reimbursement requests in the Therapy Binder while some families like to have them all together in one binder.
- Important Phone Numbers: The first page in this section can be a quick list of important numbers for this binder: pediatrician and on-call emergency numbers, health insurance number/mailing address, pharmacy numbers, laboratory numbers, poison control numbers, and so on.

The Therapy Binder

The Therapy Binder will hold all information regarding your child's long-term therapy support. This will help you keep track of plans that have worked in the past that you may want to access again, and can help you understand the ebb and flow of some of your child's challenges as well as consistent strategies that work! Here are some of the things you might have in the Therapy Binder:

- Early Intervention Paperwork: Copies of original evaluations and suggested supports, copies of all agency and therapist contact numbers, and copy of current EI therapy schedule.
- Speech and/or Occupational Therapy: Information on services, current supports and exercises, ideas of things to try at home to support speech development and sensory input.
- Cognitive Behavioral Therapy (CBT): Copies of all CBT strategies and plans, visual aids for changing thoughts and behaviors. These can be great to access and use periodically, as many sensory kids need to rotate plans and systems to help keep things new and exciting. You also may have a few strategies that work so well that they can be used in many different situations.
- Applied Behavioral Analysis (ABA): Again, copies of all ABA strategies, lists of behaviors you have supported, and the reinforcement systems that were the strongest in creating behavior changes.
- Psychiatrists: Any paperwork or information related to a possible diagnosis, medicinal support, or long-term support for your sensory child's profile can go in here.
- Neuropsychologists: This section will hold all neuropsychological evaluations complete with your child's history, current test results, current diagnoses, and current educational strategies. Some families find this section works better in their child's Education binder.
- Social Situation Cards and Social Rules: This binder can be a great place to hold any social tools you have created for your sensory child. This section could hold Social Situation or Social Nuance cards you have made (see chapter 10) and/or any social rule visual aids. Again, since many sensory kids have a hard time applying

information to different experiences, you may need to access the same social information for many experiences. You could also include here any information about social skills training classes, groups, or other resources so you have them on hand if needed.

- Important Phone Numbers: Again, the first page in this section can be a quick list of important regular and emergency numbers for all doctors, therapists, and other professionals.

Now that we have medical and therapy paperwork in place, let's look at ways we can advocate and support our sensory kids around medications and supplements.

Managing Medications and Supplements

Worksheets

The next piece of information that can be very overwhelming for families supporting sensory kids is managing medications and supplements that aim to alleviate some of the symptoms. In particular, medications can be a scary piece of parenting a sensory child, but as with many other things, if you have a checklist to help you ask the right questions, get accurate information, and know what to look for during a trial period, you will feel more in control of this process.

Many sensory kids have to try a few medications or supplements before finding the right one, and many sensory kids will need different options as their bodies grow, symptoms change or improve, and side effects get in the way. A running record of medications and supplements can be helpful for many reasons:

- Can help you, the parent, through the process of trying a new medication or supplement.
- Will give you a history of medications and supplements you have tried and why they have or have not worked for your child.
- As new medications and supplements come out, you will have information on what current medications and supplements have done to support your child and ideas of how they could be better.

Here is an example of a Medication and Supplement Worksheet:

Medication and Supplement Worksheet

Name of Medication or Supplement: ____________________

Date Started: ____________ Date Stopped: ____________

Dosage Amount: ____________________

How and when to take medication or supplement: ____________

Prescribing Doctor: ____________________

Symptom(s) you are hoping to address: ____________________

____

Initial Side Effects and how long should those last: ____________

____

Long-term Side Effects: ____________________

If this medication or supplement is working, we should see this: ____

____

Signs that my child is having an adverse reaction to the medication or supplement and should stop taking immediately are: ____________

____

I should call the prescribing doctor if: ____________________

____

Doctor contact number: office, emergency, and cell phone number

____

How often will we talk to discuss effectiveness of medication or supplement: ____________________

____

What do we do if we miss a dose: ____________________

Precautions and Drug Interactions to be aware of: ____________

____

Summary of my child's experience with this medication or supplement: ____________________

____

Keeping a record of these forms in your medical binder will help you manage your child's medications and supplements and help you see what the best supports are for your child.

Pill Organizers

If your child takes multiple medications and supplements to support their symptoms and health, it can be very important to create a system around making sure pills are taken at the right time and not missed. One way to do this is to get a few weekly pill organizers and set them up around your child's medication and supplement schedule. Once labeled appropriately, these will greatly reduce the guesswork and the remembering for you and for your child.

Here is an example of a medication or supplement system that could be used (can be adjusted based on number of times a day medications or supplements are needed): Use three pill containers labeled "Morning—with Breakfast," "Afternoon—After School," and Nighttime—with Dinner." These are kept in the kitchen around where most meals are eaten for a visual reminder and easy access.

Here's how a system like this will help you and your child:

- You can sit down once and week and set up pill cases for the week. Sunday nights are good since it is the natural "get ready for the week" night. As your child gets older, he can be a part of this process also.
- Filling pill containers weekly will give you an early heads-up on prescription renewals and reordering of supplements, which will save you the aggravation of last-minute calls to the doctor for refills or last-minute trips to the store.
- This will help you take pills on the road as needed: for dinners out at restaurants, for daylong events, and to leave at home for babysitters.
- This system also works great for traveling as long as you bring the original bottles with extras that you store somewhere else in case pill cases are lost.
- This also is a helpful tool if your child goes for a sleepover at a friend's or family member's house. This alleviates the anxiety for other parents over dispensing medications or supplements since they are clearly organized and marked. Be sure that all medications are stored safely and out of the reach of young children.

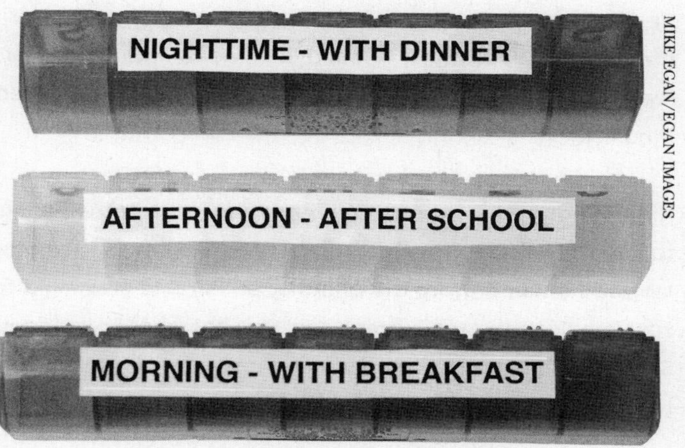

MIKE EGAN/EGAN IMAGES

Having a process in place when trying new medications or supplements and a system for organizing pills to be sure they are taken as directed can be a huge support for you and your child as you manage this piece of their care and health. Systems around medications and supplements will help you feel more in control, will help you let go of worry and anxiety around this, and free you up to be more present with your sensory child and the rest of your family.

Managing Medications at School

Some kids are going to need to take medications during the school day so you may need to create some systems for yourself and for your child's school to ensure this is done correctly. According to the American Academy of Pediatrics, there are some standard guidelines among most school districts for how to properly manage medication:

Required paperwork: When working with prescription medication, most schools require a written statement from a parent and the child's pediatrician that provides the name of the drug, the dose, approximate time it is to be taken, and the diagnosis or reason the medication is needed. Be sure to keep a copy of this form for your records (in the medication section of your Medical Binder).

Right meds in the right container: It is the parents' responsibility to supply the school with prescribed medications in the original labeled container from the pharmacist. Parents also need to be sure medications are current and that the supply is adequate. Set up an electronic or traditional paper calendar reminder system for yourself.

Administering medications: If there is not always a trained medical professional at school, it is important that the person administering the medication is trained on how to give it correctly. Make sure you know the protocol the school uses to train for the administering of medications.

Safety storage: Your child's school should have a system in place for safely storing medications.

Documentation: Schools should have a system in place that documents the administering of medications as a protocol to prevent errors and as a compliance system to share with parents. This could be a written log or a computerized student record system. Be sure you know what type of system is being used and how you can get access for regular check-ins.

Navigating the IEP and the 504 Plan

One of the most important ways we advocate for our sensory children is making sure they are getting the right support and accommodations at school. There are some tips in chapter 12 on working with and supporting your sensory child's teacher, and in this chapter we will investigate the Individualized Education Plan (IEP) and the 504 Plan, as defined below. There are so many sensory kids who need support at school, and this leaves many parents having to fight for what their child deserves and is entitled to get at school. Some parents get so frustrated with the process that they let services fall by the wayside. But once you have a basic understanding, map out your plan, and have a system in place to verify that needs are being met, it all becomes much more manageable.

This section will give you a basic understanding of the IEP (Individualized Education Program) and the 504 Plan. I will share a simplified explanation of the difference between the two, help with organizing all the special education paperwork, and suggest when it might be time to hire a special needs educational advocate or attorney. This is a highly technical and complex issue. Regulations regarding the implementation of the relevant laws differ from state to state, within a state, and from school district to school district. (See the list of references in the back of the book for further information.)

Understanding the IEP and 504 Plan

Special education for children with disabilities was first mandated by federal law in 1975 with the passage of the Education for All Handicapped Children Act. Today, there are two main pathways available to accommodate your sensory child's educational needs—the Individualized Education Plan (IEP) and the 504 Plan. The Individualized Education Plan is specifically required for all students between the ages of three and twenty-one who qualify for special education and related services under the Individuals with Disabilities Education Act (IDEA).

In contrast, the 504 Plan is mandated through the Rehabilitation Act of 1973 (The "Rehab Act"), a civil rights law whose main goal is to protect individuals with disabilities against discrimination in all areas of life based on their disability. Section 504 is managed by the U.S. Office of Civil Rights. Whereas the IEP requires that accommodations are put into place to support the needs of students with disabilities, the 504 Plan is in place to ensure that students with disabilities get access to the same educational experience as their peers.

The IEP

Wright's Law (www.wrightslaw.com), is a special education advocacy organization that gives parents, educators, advocates, and attorneys access to resources on special education law and advocacy for children with disabilities. According to Wright's Law, the main goal of IDEA is to ensure that children with disabilities have access to a free and appropriate public education that emphasizes special education and related services designed to meet their unique educational needs.

To determine if a child is eligible for services under IDEA, an evaluation is provided at no cost to parents, is performed by a multidisciplinary team, and, according to the language from IDEA, "the child is assessed in all areas related to the suspected disability." Three criteria must be met before a child becomes eligible for services: 1) an evaluation was completed, 2) the evaluation has demonstrated the child has a disability, and 3) the child's learning is impacted by the disability. Once a disability is determined, according to IDEA, a child is entitled to a Free and Appropriate Public Education (FAPE) in the Least Restrictive Environment (LRE) and, based on the child's needs, this can range from 30 minutes of related services per week to a full-time placement in an alternative setting. IDEA defines "related services" as "developmental, corrective, and other supportive services as are required to assist a child with a disability to benefit from special education" and some of the services considered include audiology, counseling or psychological, physical therapy, occupational therapy, and speech-language pathology services.

The IEP documents the specific education plan and services for each individual child (ages three to twenty-one) who has qualified for special education and related services under IDEA. The IEP specifies the educational setting they will be in, the services they will receive weekly, and the goals for the child's progress. According to IDEA, school districts receive a percentage of the cost for special education and related services provided. IEPs are mandated for an annual review to assess the services provided and progress toward the child's goals, and to determine what services will be provided for the next school year and/or the school year and the summer period that precedes it. This mandate includes the requirement that educators and service providers meet with parents to review updates to the IEP. Additionally, parents have the right to call a meeting at any time to review questions or progress against IEP goals.

The 504 Plan

The 504 Plan derives from Section 504 of the Rehab Act. Remember that the 504 is not designed to provide special education or related services; it is designed only to provide access. For this reason, some children with a mental or physical impairment do not qualify for special education services under IDEA. The 504 Plan also starts with a team determining eligibility, but the requirements for the 504 Plan are less stringent than those for IDEA, and focus on making reasonable accommodations and modifications in the regular education environment and to the regular curriculum to meet the child's needs. Like the IEP, the 504 Plan is a legal document, and though there is no mandated annual review, most school districts do meet with parents annually to evaluate progress and plan for the coming school year. If a parent feels that the accommodations in a current 504 Plan are not working, they can request a meeting to review and rewrite the 504 Plan's accommodations for their child.

Important Differences

According to an article from the Wright's Law website, "Section 504 and IDEA: Basic Similarities and Differences" by John S. Rosenfeld, there are some important differences to highlight between IDEA and the Section 504 of the Rehab Act.

The purpose of Section 504 is to "level the playing field" to avoid exclusion of children with disabilities. The purpose of IDEA is to provide additional programs and services to children with disabilities, programs that are not available to students without disabilities. Under IDEA, school districts are eligible for additional, though minimal, funding to support the special education and related services that are provided to eligible students. Because Section 504 is focused on protecting students with disabilities from discrimination and providing access to equal education through accommodations or modifications, no additional funding is provided. This can leave some parents feeling that school districts have little incentive to support their child under a 504 plan.

A school district's obligations are more clearly spelled out under IDEA, and because this statute includes a process to settle complaints, the school district is more accountable for enforcing the agreed upon special education and related services.

Understanding Special Education Law and its impact on your child's education is a very complex process and this section just gives you a very general outline to get started. That being said, it may be important that you have a broader understanding of the differences between the 504 Plan and the IEP so you can work with your school district to try to create the right learning environment for your child. (For further special education information, please see the Resources section in the back of the book.)

Education Binder: Organized Information Can Mean Better Services

One of the best ways to support yourself in this process of navigating the IEP and the 504 Plan is to have an Education Binder for your child. This would hold all things connected to your child's learning, school evaluations, and IEP or 504 Plan paperwork.

An Education Binder might include the following sections:

- Important Phone Numbers: Again, the first page in this section can be a quick list of important numbers for this binder, including numbers and/or emails for your child's school, teacher, special education teacher, speech, OT, school psychologist, special education coordinator for your school department, superintendent, and numbers for special education advocates if needed.

- Report Cards: A history of your child's report cards and teacher comments in chronological order. This can help you see patterns in subjects or times of year that impact your child's learning.
- Examples of Work: It can also be helpful to have some samples of your child's work, examples of when your child was working at his/her best and some when your child was most challenged.
- Journal: Here's a great place to journal what is going on. List dates and examples of things that are not working, or not being done, as well as examples of supports and services that are working.
- School-based Evaluations: Copies of any school-based evaluations.
- IEP or 504 Plan Documents: This section would hold copies, in chronological order, of any annual IEP meeting, special IEP meetings, and 504 Plan meetings. This will give you one place to go to access what your child is currently eligible for and what accommodations and modifications are being used to support your child.
- Notes from any IEP or 504 Plan Meetings: This is a critical part for parents. Taking good notes at each IEP or 504 Plan meeting can help you be sure the right services and accommodations are being implemented as planned. Because schools are usually supporting many kids on IEPs and 504 Plans, good follow-up is an important aspect of advocating for your sensory child.
- Copies of specific pages of IDEA 2004 or Section 504 that clarify important definitions or pertain to specific challenges you have encountered with your school district.

Without a doubt, having a system that organizes your child's current IEP or 504 Plan paperwork, has notes from all your meetings with the school team, and evaluations to reference will help you get the best services for your child.

Special-Needs Educational Advocates and Attorneys

Unfortunately, for some parents, there comes a time when they feel like their child's needs are not being met despite frequent meetings and evaluations. At this point, some parents feel the need to hire an advocate or an attorney to help them get their child the services they are legally entitled to and/or get them placed in an alternative setting because of inadequate services.

The best place to start when you are at this point is to contact an educational advocate or attorney who specializes in this area. Many offer a free consultation to review the law and your child's needs to see if there is a breach in the law and what your school is legally mandated to provide for your child. A great resource is the Council of Parent Attorneys and Advocates, www.copaa.org, a national membership association dedicated to securing high-quality educational services for children with disabilities. They have a list, by state, of attorneys and advocates.

Slow and Steady

As with so many other things we have talked about throughout this book, advocating for your child at school might be a long-term process. You are going to need to have a good sense of how your child is doing at school, what services and accommodations are working, and what needs tweaking. Because the learning process is an ever growing and changing experience, we also need to evolve the supports we utilize during this process.

The most important thing you can have in place for your child is your utmost belief in their innate strengths. You will need to celebrate and highlight your child's successes but always be ready for the next challenge. It is this realistic coaching, along with the external organizing supports we have created, that will set you and your child up for long-term success.

Conclusion

My Hopes for Your Sensory Organizing Experience

As sensory parents, we've all known the frustration, sense of helplessness, and heartache that comes with seeing our kids struggle at home and in the world. I hope that this book and my sensory organizing techniques have helped you begin to imagine a new, more peaceful, and connected life for you, your sensory child, and your entire family. I hope you can now imagine mornings, afternoons, and evenings that run more peacefully as your sensory child seamlessly transitions from one task to another, thanks to the roadmap of the structure, routines, and visual guides you've put in place.

We've learned that even though sensory kids might have different diagnoses, they often share universal strengths and similar core challenges. No matter what the diagnoses or challenges, the SSK Sensory Organizing Worksheet helps us slow down, become an objective observer, tap into how our sensory child learns best, and prioritize what our child needs today. These tools give you the power to create the right supports that will enhance your child's daily experiences.

Now you know how to create an environment in your home that counterbalances the innate challenges your sensory child navigates daily—something that will help them feel loved and understood. Having sensory designed spaces, as well as clear visual aids, structure, and set routines around challenging times and tasks, will give your child the external map they need to navigate life at home successfully: a gift for your entire family. We also learned that many of these strategies can be applied to helping your child in the world. We can now provide a roadmap for those overwhelming experiences, from the birthday party to the first day of school, giving us a great teaching opportunity that helps our sensory kids learn how to successfully navigate the world outside the home.

We have also embraced the power of the Golden Tool in supporting everything you, your sensory child, and your family experiences. By learning how to observe, identify the challenge, break things into smaller pieces, and create a focused tool, we are bringing a small piece of mindfulness into our families' daily experience. We are building confidence through success and supporting the here and now with unconditional love.

Lastly, I hope that this book has helped you shift into a place of seeing, feeling, and experiencing the infinite joy that can come from raising a rigid, anxious, or distracted child. Our sensory kids bring unique gifts to us, to our families, and to everyone they touch. As parents, they give us the opportunity to challenge ourselves to be better as we help our children thrive.

Now it's your time to bring out the best in your child, and you have all the tools you need to get started. You have always been the best advocate for your child. No one knows him better or cares more. With the Sensory Organizing principles described in this book, you have a detailed system that empowers you, your child, and your entire family to thrive and to find new levels of acceptance and happiness. I wish you all the best on your sensory journey.

Resources

Further Reading

Sensory Processing Disorder

Carol Stock Kranowitz. *The Out-of-Sync Child: Recognizing and Coping with Sensory Processing Disorder*, rev. ed. New York: Perigee, 2005.

______. *The Out-of-Sync Child Has Fun: Activities for Kids with Sensory Processing Disorder*, rev. ed. New York: Perigee, 2006.

Lindsey Biel and Nancy Peske. *Raising a Sensory Smart Child: The Definitive Handbook for Helping Your Child with Sensory Processing Issues.* New York: Penguin, 2009.

Lucy Jane Miller. *Sensational Kids: Hope and Help for Children with Sensory Processing Disorder.* New York: Putnam, 2006.

Tara Delaney. *The Sensory Processing Disorder Answer Book: Practical Answers to the Top 250 Questions Parents Ask.* Naperville: Sourcebooks, 2008.

Attention Deficit/Hyperactivity Disorder

Russell A. Barkley. *Taking Charge of ADHD: The Complete, Authoritative Guide for Parents*, rev. ed. New York: Guilford Press, 2000.

Edward M. Hallowell and John J. Ratey. *Driven to Distraction: Recognizing and Coping with Attention Deficit Disorder from Childhood Through Adulthood*, fifth ed. New York: Touchstone, 1995.

Edward M. Hallowell and Peter S. Jensen. *Superparenting for ADD: An Innovative Approach to Raising Your Distracted Child.* New York: Ballantine Books, 2008.

Vincent J. Monastra. *Parenting Children with ADHD: 10 Lessons That Medicine Cannot Teach.* Washington: American Psychological Association, 2005.

Anxiety Disorder

Tamar E. Chansky. *Freeing Your Child from Anxiety: Powerful, Practical Solutions to Overcome Your Child's Fears, Worries, and Phobias.* New York: Three Rivers Press, 2004.

Ronald M. Rapee, Ann Wignall, Vanessa Cobham, Susan Spence, and Heidi Lyneham. *Helping Your Anxious Child: A Step-by-Step Guide for Parents,* second ed. Oakland: New Harbinger Publications, 2008.

John S. Dacey and Lisa B. Fiore. *Your Anxious Child: How Parents and Teachers Can Relieve Anxiety in Children.* San Francisco: Jossey Bass, 2001.

Tamar E. Chansky. *Freeing Your Child from Obsessive-Compulsive Disorder: A Powerful, Practical Program for Parents of Children and Adolescents.* New York: Three Rivers Press, 2001.

Autism Spectrum Disorders and Asperger's

Chantal Sicile-Kira, with foreword by Temple Grandin. *Autism Spectrum Disorders: The Complete Guide to Understanding Autism, Asperger's Syndrome, Pervasive Developmental Disorder, and Other ASDs.* New York: Perigee, 2004.

Ellen Notbohm and Veronica Zysk, with foreword by Temple Grandin. *1001 Great Ideas for Teaching and Raising Children with Autism or Asperger's,* rev. second ed. Arlington, Texas: Future Horizons, 2010.

Tony Attwood. *The Complete Guide to Asperger's Syndrome.* London and Philadelphia: Jessica Kingsley, 2008.

Elaine Hall and Diane Isaacs. *Seven Keys to Unlock Autism: Making Miracles in the Classroom.* San Francisco: Jossey Bass, 2011.

Mood Disorders, including Bipolar Disorder

Ross W. Greene. *The Explosive Child: A New Approach for Understanding and Parenting Easily Frustrated, Chronically Inflexible Children,* second ed. New York: Harper Paperbacks, 2001.

Tracy Anglada and Sheryl Hakala. *The Childhood Bipolar Disorder Answer Book: Practical Answers to the Top 300 Questions Parents Ask.* Naperville: Sourcebooks Inc., 2008.

Judith Lederman and Candida Fink. *The Ups and Downs of Raising a Bipolar Child: A Survival Guide for Parents.* New York: Touchstone, 2003.

Pat Harvey and Jeanine Penzo. *Parenting a Child Who Has Intense Emotions: Dialectical Behavior Therapy Skills to Help Your Child Regulate Emotional Outbursts and Aggressive Behaviors.* Oakland: New Harbinger Publications, 2009.

Social and Emotional Skills

Carol Gray. *The New Social Story Book, Revised and Expanded 10th Anniversary Edition: Over 150 Social Stories That Teach Everyday Social Skills to Children with Autism or Asperger's Syndrome, and Their Peers,* revised ed. Arlington, Texas: Future Horizons, 2010.

Michelle Garcia Winner. *Thinking About You, Thinking About Me,* second ed. San Jose: Think Social Publishing, 2007.

Richard Lavoie. *It's So Much Work to Be Your Friend: Helping the Child with Learning Disabilities Find Social Success.* New York: Touchstone, 2005.

Stephanie Madrigal and Michelle Garcia Winner. *Superflex . . . A Superhero Social Thinking Curriculum.* San Jose: Think Social, 2008.

Brenda Smith Myles, Melissa L. Trautman, and Ronda L. Schelvan. *The Hidden Curriculum: Practical Solutions for Understanding Unstated Rules in Social Situations.* Shawnee Mission, Kansas: Autism Asperger Publishing Company, 2004.

Executive Function

Peg Dawson and Richard Guare. *Smart but Scattered: The Revolutionary "Executive Skills" Approach to Helping Kids Reach Their Potential.* New York: Guilford Press, 2009.

Joyce Cooper-Kahn and Laurie Dietzel. *Late, Lost, and Unprepared: A Parents' Guide to Helping Children with Executive Functioning.* Bethesda, Maryland: Woodbine House, 2008.

Donna Goldberg with Jennifer Zwiebel. *The Organized Student: Teaching Children the Skills for Success in School and Beyond.* New York: Touchstone, 2005.

Martin L. Kutscher and Marcella Moran. *Organizing the Disorganized Child: Simple Strategies to Succeed in School.* New York: William Morrow Paperbacks, 2009.

PANDAS, OCD, and Lyme Disease

Beth Alison Maloney. *Saving Sammy: Curing the Boy Who Caught OCD.* New York: Crown Publishing, 2009.

Tamar E. Chansky. *Freeing Your Child from Obsessive-Compulsive Disorder: A Powerful, Practical Program for Parents of Children and Adolescents.* New York: Three Rivers Press, 2001.

Aureen Pinto Wagner. *What to Do When Your Child Has Obsessive-Compulsive Disorder: Strategies and Solutions.* Mobile: Lighthouse Press, Inc., 2002.

Denise Lang. *Coping with Lyme Disease: A Practical Guide to Dealing with Diagnosis and Treatment,* third ed. New York: Holt Paperbacks, 2004.

Pamela Weintraub. *Cure Unknown: Inside the Lyme Epidemic.* New York: St. Martin's Griffin, 2009.

IEP and 504 Support

Linda Wilmshurst and Alan W. Brue. *The Complete Guide to Special Education: Expert Advice on Evaluations, IEPs, and Helping Kids Succeed,* second ed. San Francisco: Jossey-Bass, 2010.

Lawrence M. Siegel. *The Complete IEP Guide: How to Advocate for Your Special Ed Child*, seventh ed. Berkeley: NOLO, 2011.

Peter W. D. Wright and Pamela Darr Wright. *Wrightslaw: From Emotions to Advocacy: The Special Education Survival Guide*, second ed. Hartfield, Virginia: Harbor House Law Press, 2010.

Rich Weinfeld and Michelle Davis. *Special Needs Advocacy Resource Book: What You Can Do Now to Advocate for Your Exceptional Child's Education.* Austin: Prufrock Press, 2008.

Sibling Support

Donald J. Meyer and Patricia F. Vadasy. *Sibshops: Workshops for Siblings of Children with Special Needs.*

Kate Strohm. *Being the Other One: Growing Up with a Brother or Sister Who Has Special Needs.* Boston: Shambhala, 2005.

Lorraine Donlon. *The Other Kid: A Draw It Out Guide for Kids Dealing with a Special Needs Sibling.* Tamarac: Llumina Kids, 2011.

Sensory Travel Support

Deb Wills and Debra Koma. *PassPorter's Walt Disney World for Your Special Needs: The Take-Along Travel Guide and Planner.* Ann Arbor: PassPorter Travel Pass, 2005.

Loris Bree and Marlin Bree. *Kid's Trip Diary: Kids! Write About Your Own Adventures and Experiences.* St. Paul: Marlor Press, 2007.

General Organizing Books

Peter Walsh. *It's All Too Much: An Easy Plan for Living a Richer Life with Less Stuff.* New York: Free Press, 2006.

Julie Morgenstern. *Organizing From the Inside Out.* New York: Holt, 1998.

______. *SHED Your Stuff, Change Your Life: A Four-Step Guide to Getting Unstuck.* New York: Touchstone, 2009.

Lorie Marrero. *The Clutter Diet: The Skinny on Organizing Your Home and Taking Control* of Your Life. Austin, TX: Reason Press, 2009.

Memoirs by Parents Raising Sensory Kids

Priscilla Gilman. *The Anti-Romantic Child.* New York: HarperCollins, 2011.

Shonda Schilling. *The Best Kind of Different: Our Family's Journey with Asperger's Syndrome.* New York: William Morrow Press, 2012.

Products I Love

Sensory Organizing Products

Stores That Help Us Create Sensory Systems

Many of the sensory systems talked about in this book represent products that can be found at office supply stores, home stores, organizing stores, and school supply stores. Here is a list of each of these categories.

Office Supply Stores

Staples: www.staples.com.
Office Max: www.officemax.com.
Office Depot: www.officedepot.com.

Home Stores

IKEA: www.ikea.com.
Target: www.target.com.
Walmart: www.walmart.com.
Bed, Bath, and Beyond: www.bedbathbeyond.com.
Pottery Barn, Pottery Barn Kids, Pottery Barn Teen: www.potterybarn.com.

Organizing and DIY Home Stores

Container Store: www.containerstore.com.
Lowe's: www.lowes.com.
Home Depot: www.homedepot.com.

School Supplies Stores

Lakeshore Learning: www.lakeshorelearning.com.

Learning Resources: www.learningresources.com.

Teacher Created Resources: www.teachercreated.com.

Sensory Product Retailers

Southpaw Enterprises: www.southpawenterprises.com.

Sensory Edge: www.sensoryedge.com.

Therapro: www.therapro.com.

Fun and Function: www.funandfunction.com.

Chapter-by-Chapter Sensory Product List

In the effort to break down and organize this process for you, I have also created a chapter-by-chapter product list to help you find what you need to support your sensory child! Links to some products can be found at www.thesensorychildgetsorganized.com/Products_That_Help.htm.

Chapter 3: How Does Your Child Learn Best?

Notebooks and Journal Books

Martha Stewart Home Office with Avery—notebooks, journals, and calendars—www.avery.com/avery/en_us/Products/Martha-Stewart-Home-Office-with-Avery.

Office Supply Stores

Apps for Calendar Journaling for Mood Disorders, Depression, Anxiety

Optimism Apps: www.findingoptimism.com.

Mood Panda: moodpanda.com.

iTunes Apps: Mood Tracking Diary, Moody Me: Mood Diary and Tracker, itunes.apple.com.

T2 Mood Tracker, eMoods Bipolar Mood Tracker, Mood Journal Plus for Android: www.android.com/apps.

Chapter 5: The Fundamentals of Sensory Spaces

Label Products

Avery—www.avery.com. Martha Stewart Home Office with Avery—www.avery.com/avery/en_us/Products/Martha-Stewart-Home-Office-with-Avery.

Picture Image Symbols for Labels

Boardmaker: www.mayer-johnson.com/boardmaker-software.

DynaVox Mayer-Johnson, 2100 Wharton Street, Suite 400, Pittsburgh, PA 15203. Phone: (800) 588-4548. Fax: (866) 585-6260 Email: mayer-johnson.usa@www.mayer-johnson.com. Website: mayer-johnson.com.

Picture Exchange Communication System (PECS)—www.pecsusa.com/

Do to Learn: Educational Resources for Special Needs: www.do2learn.com.

Chill-Out Zone

Yogibo—bean bag furniture—www.yogibo.com.

Weighted Products and Sensory Handheld Toys

Southpaw Enterprises: www.southpawenterprises.com.

Therapro: www.therapro.com.

IKEA: www.ikea.com, for the KURA reversible bed and the KURA bed tent.

Vic Firth Kidphones: www.vicfirth.com.

Chapter 6: Sensory Organizing and Storage Systems for the Bedroom

Storage Bins

Clear Lego Bin: Sterilite 15-quart and 2.7-quart plus many other sizes, www.sterilite.com.

Clothes Organization

IKEA: www.ikea.com.

Trofast Storage System

Clear Closet Bins: Sterilite Deep Stacking Bin, www.sterilite.com.

Vertical Sweater Organizers: 6-Shelf Organizer: Michael Graves for Target, www.target.com.

Row of Hooks, Garment Hook: Lowe's, www.lowes.com.

Stuffed Animal Storage

Animal Bag by Boon: an animal storage bag that doubles as a snuggly seat: perfect for sensory kids who won't let go of stuffed animals, www.booninc.com/products/AnimalBag/393.

IKEA PS FÅNGST hanging storage: six compartments: great for stuffed animals or other light items, www.ikea.com/us/en/catalog/products/70115578.

Seam and Tag Sensitivities

Undercover Tape: adhesive fabric strips that help sensory sensitivities to seams and labels, www.mimilounge.com.

Wall of Success

Magnetic Chalkboard Paint, Magnamagic: www.magnamagic.com.

Cork Tiles and Magnetic Dry-Erase Tile Boards: Board Dudes, www.boarddudes.com.

Sensory Sleeping Spaces

Lycra Bed Sheet: www.laceandfabric.com.

Weighted Blankets and Products: Southpaw Enterprises, www.southpawenterprises.com, or Therapro, www.therapro.com.

Important note: Check with your child's OT for guidelines on using the correct amount of weight and for the proper length of time to use weighted products with your child.

Bedside Organizers: Get it Together Bedside Caddy: Walmart, www.walmart.com.

Zazoo Photo Clock: www.zazookids.com. Help your child develop healthy sleep patterns by using images/photos to help children understand "time to wake up" and "time to stay in bed."

Chapter 7: Creating a Fun and Functional Playroom

Active Zone

Circo Toy Tote with Wheels: Target, www.target.com.

Everlast Blockers and Mini Trampoline: Sports Authority, www.sportsauthority.com.

Disk Seat: Isokinetics, www.isokineticsinc.com.

IKEA Ekorre Swing: IKEA, www.ikea.com.

Doorway Swings: eSpecial Needs, www.eSpecialNeeds.com.

Lounge and Bean Bag Furniture: YOGIBO super-comfy and supportive lounge bean bag furniture: from big lounge bags to neck wraps and everything in between, www.yogibo.com.

Quiet Zone

Weighted Products: Southpaw Enterprises, www.southpawenterprises.com, and Therapro, www.therapro.com.

Noise-blocking Kidphones: Vic Firth, www.vicfirth.com.

Art Zone

Table: Room Essentials Coffee Table: Target, www.target.com.

Drawer Systems, Crayon Box, and Under-the-Bed Storage Bin to use as Rice Bin, www.sterilite.com.

Building Zone and Free Toy Zone

Lego Bin, plastic drawer bin unit on wheels: Sterilite, www.sterilite.com.

Trofast Storage System would work here also: www.ikea.com.

ClosetMaid Cubeicals: cube organizers with cloth bins, www.closetmaid.com.

Chapter 8: Connect with Your Child

Feelings

Feelings Book, by Emily Rubin and Amy Laurent. Communication Crossroads, www.commxroads.com.

"Feelings Book" App for iPhone, iPad, iPod Touch: www.itunes.apple.com/us/app/feelings-book.

Kimochi Mini Mixed Bag of Feelings Tube with Key Chain: Great for younger sensory kids to help them learn and identify their feelings, www.shop.kimochis.com.

Central Message Area

Weekly and Monthly Calendars

Monthly Wall Calendar: Day Runner Monthly Wall Calendar by Mead, www.meadonline.com.

3M Post-it Weekly Calendar. This is a weekly paper calendar with four sections that can be used for different family members or used for different categories. The color-coded sticky notes allow you to move around calendar items easily: great for setting up and readjusting the weekly plan! www.post-it.com.

Board Dudes Weekly Aluminum Framed Whiteboard Calendar or Board Dudes Weekly Whiteboard planner with Cork Strip, www.boarddudes.com.

Framed Cork Board, www.boarddudes.com.

Smaller Weekly Whiteboard Calendars

Martha Stewart Dry Erase Weekly Planner, www.avery.com or www.staples.com.

Command Plastic Hooks: damage-free hanging solutions, www.command.com.

Same Time, Same Place

Time Timer and Mobile Time Timer Apps, also: www.timetimer.com.

Homework Bins and Caddies

Small plastic bins with lock tops: www.sterilite.com.

Caddy for homework, bathroom supplies, hair supplies: Lakeshore Learning, www.lakeshorelearning.com.

Small White Board (8.5" x 11") for Planning Homework and Get Ready Schedule: Board Dudes, www.boarddudes.com.

Visual Aids

Pocket Charts for Checklists: Learning Center Pocket Charts (set of six): Lakeshore Learning, www.lakeshorelearning.com.

Mini Pocket Charts: great for holding Chore Cards or other smaller visual aids, www.lakeshorelearning.com.

Picture Schedule Charts: "Choiceworks" Visual Support System: image charts that provide framework for creating schedules and giving choices around transitions. Also an app available for iPhone, iTouch, and iPad, www.beevisual.com.

Laminating Services

Individual laminating services as well as laminating machines for home can be found at office supply stores.

Social Stories

Carol Gray: The Gray Center, www.thegraycenter.org. *The New Social Story Book, Revised and Expanded 10th Anniversary Edition: Over 150 Social Stories that Teach Everyday Social Skills to Children with Autism or Asperger's Syndrome, and their Peers,* revised ed. Arlington, Texas: Future Horizons, 2010.

Chapter 9: Making Trouble Times Easy

Mealtime Supports

Disk Seat for Dinner (seated yet moving!) Isokinetics, www.isokineticsinc.com.

Conversation Games for Dinner Distraction: Continuum Games: Family Talk 1 and 2, Grandparent Talk, www.continuumgames.com.

Family Time Fun: Dinner Games, www.ftfgames.com.

Morning Rush

Pop-up Hamper: Target, Walmart, Kohl's.

Plastic Drawer Bin: Sterilite, www.sterilite.com.

Homework Supplies

Noise Blocking Kidphones: Vic Firth, www.vicfirth.com.

Personalized, dry-erase clipboards for kids—Frecklebox—www.frecklebox.com/Personalized-Clipboards-For-Kids.

Graphic Organizers K–3, 4–8: Teacher Created Resources, www.teachercreated.com.

Homework Bins: www.sterilite.com.

Caddies: www.lakeshorelearning.com.

Dictation System (Use with wireless headset for flexibility in moving and walking while talking): Dragon NaturallySpeaking, www.nuance.com/dragon.

Lifescribe: special pen that records everything that is said and written, www.lifescribe.com.

Chore Time

Mini Pocket Charts: Great for holding Chore Cards or other smaller visual aids, www.lakeshorelearning.com.

Laundry Sorting Bin for Whites, Medium Colors, Darks: See Home or Organizing Stores.

Chapter 10: Leaving the Nest

Social and Situational Tools

Social experience books for young children: Berenstain Bears, www.berenstainbears.com.

Apps for Social Situations: Model Me Kids, www.modelmekids.com, and Proloquo2go, www.proloquo.com.

Social Thinking: Michelle Garcia Winner, www.socialthinking.com. *You Are a Social Detective: Explaining Social Thinking to Kids,* by Michelle Garcia Winner and Pamela Crooke. Great Barrington, Mass.: North River Press Publishing Corporation, 2010.

Social Smart Kids Discussion Cards, www.socialsmartkids.com.

Comic Life: Take your own pictures and create a comic book social story and picture albums for your sensory child. PC, Mac, and iPad compatible. www.comiclife.com.

Keeping Track of Sensory Stuff

Get Your Gear Cards: visual gear card with images and words to help sensory kids pack their gear for different situations, www.simplyordered.com.

IdentaMe Labels: Personalized, durable, dishwasher safe, laundry safe, and microwave safe labels to help your sensory kids keep track of their things, www.identamelabels.com.

Mabels Labels: Personalized, waterproof name labels and tags for kids, adults, household, and seasonal items, www.mabelslabels.com.

Chapter 11: Over the River and Through the Woods

Sensory Travel Tips, Supplies, and Games

Disposable Wristbands, www.mypreciouskid.com.

Transportation Security Administration (TSA), www.tsa.gov: tips for travel with special needs children and adults. The TSA also has a helpline, TSA Cares, for individuals with special needs: 1-855-787-2227. Travelers may call with questions about screening policies, procedures, and what to expect at the security checkpoint.

Continuum Games: Great Conversation Games when traveling and visiting family and friends: Family Talk, Grandparent Talk, Teen Talk, Buddy Talk, www.continuumgames.com.

Family Fun Time Games (Dinner Games and Gather 'Round the Restaurant Game), www.ftfgames.com.

Melissa and Doug Travel Games, www.melissaanddoug.com.

Travel Activity Mat, Storage, Carryall Solution (great for small pieces like Legos, action heros, etc.): Lay-n-Go, www.layngo.com.

Kids Travel Journals: Galison/Mudpuppy, www.galison.com.

Disney Vacation Supports

Disney World, www.disneyworld.com: Disney has many vacation supports in place for children with special needs.

Disney Vacation Books: *PassPorter's Walt Disney World for Your Special Needs: The Take-Along Travel Guide and Planner!*, by Deb Wills and Debra Martin Koma.

Tips and Help with Disney Vacations for Sensory Families: Ears of Experience, www.themouseexperts.com/specialneeds.

Chapter 13: Becoming an Advocate

Paperwork Systems

Binders and clear insert pages can be found at all office supply stores.

Portable File Folders

Portable Accordion File: Martha Stewart Home Office with Avery at Staples, www.staples.com.

Mail Baskets and Wall File Holders

Home Stores

Medication Pill Containers and Organizers

Medication organizers or stackable pill containers can be found at pharmacies like CVS, www.cvs.com; Rite Aid, www.riteaid.com; or Walgreens, www.walgreens.com.

Organizations That Help

Sensory Processing Disorder

The Sensory Processing Disorder Foundation

Organization working to expand knowledge, foster awareness, and promote recognition of sensory processing disorder.

www.spdfoundation.net

Sensory Processing Disorder Resource Center

To help parents, educators, and caregivers connect with information about the diagnosis, treatment, and support for sensory processing disorder.

www.sensory-processing-disorder.com

Attention Deficit/Hyperactivity Disorder

National Attention Deficit Disorder Association

The National Attention Deficit Disorder Association provides information, resources, and networking opportunities to help people with attention deficit/hyperactivity disorder lead better lives.

www.add.org

CHADD: Child and Adults with Attention Deficit/Hyperactivity Disorder

CHADD is the nation's leading nonprofit organization serving individuals with AD/HD and their families. CHADD has more than 16,000 members in 200 local chapters throughout the United States. Chapters offer support for individuals, parents, teachers, professionals, and others.

www.chadd.org

NRC: National Resource Center on ADHD

A program of CHADD, NRC was established in 2002 to be the national clearinghouse for the latest evidence-based information on AD/HD. The NRC provides comprehensive information and support to individuals with AD/HD, their families and friends, and the professionals involved in their lives.

www.help4adhd.org

ADDitude magazine

ADDitude is a leading online and print resource and magazine for families and adults living with AD/HD and learning disabilities.

www.additudemag.com

Anxiety Disorder

Anxiety Disorders Association of America (ADAA)

ADAA specializes in the advocacy, education, training, and research for anxiety and stress-related disorders.

www.adaa.org

Freedom from Fear: Anxiety and Depression Resource Organization

Freedom from Fear is a national not-for-profit mental health advocacy association. The mission of FFF is to impact, in a positive way, the lives of all those affected by anxiety, depressive, and related disorders through advocacy, education, research, and community support.

www.freedomfromfear.org

International OCD (Obsessive Compulsive Disorder) Foundation (IOCDF)

Organization that supports raising awareness, research, and resources for OCD sufferers and their families.

www.ocfoundation.org

Autism Spectrum Disorders, Including Asperger's

Autism Speaks

Autism Speaks is one of the nation's largest autism advocacy organizations with a national network of autism advocates, researchers, and parents.

www.autismspeaks.org

The Autism Society

Founded in 1965, this is a leading source of trusted and reliable information about autism.

www.autism-society.org

Generation Rescue

Generation Rescue was founded by parents Lisa and JB Handley in 2005 and joined later by Jenny McCarthy after her own journey with her autistic son. Generation Rescue is an international movement of scientists, parents, and physicians researching the causes and treatments for autism, AD/HD, and chronic illness.

www.generationrescue.org

US Autism and Asperger's Association (USAAA)

US Autism and Asperger's Association (USAAA) is a nonprofit organization that supports the autism community with education, training, accessible resources, and partnerships with local and national projects.
www.usautism.org

The Miracle Project

The Miracle Project is a multi-platform socialization program that enables children and teens with autism and other special needs to express themselves through music, dance, acting, story, and writing.
www.themiracleproject.org

Mood Disorders, Including Bipolar Disorder

Lives in the Balance

This is a nonprofit organization founded by Dr. Ross Greene (author of *The Explosive Child* and *Lost at School*) to give support to parents and caregivers who are living with and learning how to support chronically inflexible and rigid children.
www.livesinthebalance.org

The Balanced Mind Foundation

The Balanced Mind is a not-for-profit organization of families raising children and teens affected by depression, bipolar disorder, and other mood disorders.
www.thebalancedmind.org

BPChildren

BPChildren is an organization founded by Tracy Anglada, a mental health writer, advocate, and mother. The main focus of BPChildren is to provide resources to children with bipolar disorder, along with their family, friends, and teachers.
www.bpchildren.org

Social and Emotional Skills

The Gray Center for Social Understanding

The Gray Center is a nonprofit organization that cultivates the strengths of individuals with autism and those who interact with them, and globally promotes social understanding.

www.thegraycenter.org

Social Thinking

Social Thinking is a treatment framework and curriculum developed by Michelle Garcia Winner that targets improving individual social thinking abilities, regardless of diagnostic label. Professionals and parents alike are using these methods to build social thinking capacities in their students, children and adults.

www.socialthinking.com

teach2talk

Teach2Talk, LLC produces educational resources for children that target core speech, language, play, and social skills using techniques including video modeling.

www.teach2talk.com

Social Skill Builder

Social Skill Builder's series of innovative software programs use interactive videos to teach key social thinking, language, and behavior that are critical to everyday living.

www.socialskillbuilder.com

Executive Function

LD Online

Learning Disabilities (LD) Online seeks to "help children and adults reach their full potential by providing accurate and up-to-date information and advice about learning disabilities and AD/HD."

www.ldonline.org

National Center for Learning Disabilities

The National Center for Learning Disabilities (NCLD) works to ensure that the nation's 15 million children, adolescents, and adults with learning disabilities have every opportunity to succeed in school, work, and life.

www.ncld.org

Learning Disabilities Association of America (LDA)

Since 1963, LDA has provided support to people with learning disabilities, their parents, teachers and other professionals.

www.ldanatl.org

PANDAS, OCD, Lyme Disease

Lyme Disease Association, Inc.

The Lyme Disease Association (LDA) expanded its focus nationally almost a dozen years ago. It is dedicated to Lyme disease education, prevention, research funding, and patient support.

www.lymediseaseassociation.org

International Lyme and Associated Diseases Society (ILADS)

ILADS is a nonprofit, international, multidisciplinary medical society dedicated to the diagnosis and appropriate treatment of Lyme and its associated diseases.

www.ilads.org

PANDAS Network

A resource library of medical studies and case histories gathered largely by a group of twenty parents whose children had the sudden onset of PANDAS in 2007–2008.

www.pandasnetwork.org

Saving Sammy—Curing the Boy Who Caught OCD

Mom, author, and PANDAS expert Beth A. Maloney offers her services as a patient advocate and mental health consultant to parents and

caregivers across the country. She also has a tool kit that provides you with concrete steps you can take to work with your doctor in improving your child's health.
www.savingsammy.net

Children's Lyme Disease Network

An all-volunteer organization consisting of parents, caregivers, and family members who have seen firsthand the struggles a child can face once infected with Lyme disease.
www.childrenslymenetwork.org

Special Education and Related Services: IEP and 504 Support

Wrightslaw Special Education Law and Advocacy

Wrightslaw is a leading website about special education law and advocacy, with thousands of articles, cases, and free resources. Parents, educators, advocates, and attorneys come to Wrightslaw for accurate, reliable information about special education law, education law, and advocacy for children with disabilities.
www.wrightslaw.com

Council of Parent Attorneys and Advocates (COPAA)

COPAA is a national membership association dedicated to securing high-quality educational services for children with disabilities. They have a list, by state, of attorneys and advocates who support children with disabilities.
www.copaa.org

See executive function section for additional resources on learning disabilities.

Sibling Support

Sibling Support Project

The Sibling Support Project is a national effort dedicated to the lifelong concerns of brothers and sisters of people who have special health, developmental, or mental health concerns.

www.siblingsupport.org

There are special-needs organizations, hospitals, and other organizations that run sibling support groups all over the country. Be sure to check your area.

Sensory Travel Support

Ears of Experience: Exceptional Disney Trips for Exceptional Children

A travel-planning service that specializes in planning Disney vacations for special-needs kids.

www.themouseexperts.com/specialneeds.html

Transportation Security Administration (TSA)

Tips on air travel with children with special needs.

www.tsa.gov/travelers/airtravel/specialneeds/editorial_1572.shtm

Other Organizations That Help Sensory Kids and Their Families

American Academy of Child and Adolescent Psychiatry

www.aacap.org

The American Academy of Pediatrics

www.aap.org

National Alliance for the Mentally Ill (NAMI)

NAMI is the nation's largest grassroots mental health organization dedicated to building better lives for the millions of Americans affected

by mental illness. NAMI advocates for access to services, treatment, supports, and research and is steadfast in its commitment to raising awareness and building a community of hope for all of those in need.
www.nami.org

Federation of Families for Children's Mental Health (FFCMH)
ffcmh.org

Peacelove Studios (PLS)

PeaceLove Studios was founded by an OCD sufferer who found peace of mind though art. PeaceLove was established to build the first positive symbol for mental illness, create expressive arts programming to help people find peace of mind, and build inclusive spaces where communities could come together to experience storytelling, expressive arts, and cool products that inspire a positive lifestyle.
www.peacelovestudios.com

Parents Helping Parents

Parent-directed family resource center for children with special needs.
php.com

ResilientKids

ResilientKids offers an innovative yoga and mindfulness curricula that works directly with students in their school setting. This secular program is designed to promote the development of lifelong skills, including focus, self-esteem, self-confidence, balance, and community.
www.resilientkids.org

Acknowledgments

I need to start off by thanking the many parents and children who let me into their homes to help them learn how to use Sensory Organizing techniques. It is one thing to go visit a doctor or therapist at his or her office to ask for help, but it is an entirely different thing to let someone into your home to see everything exactly as it is. This willingness to be vulnerable allowed the families I work with to make amazing shifts into a place of acceptance and understanding of new Sensory Organizing rules. Also, it was through these interactions with my clients and their families that I continued to grow, refine, and enhance the SSK Sensory Organizing strategies. Their courage now manifests itself through the pages in this book and will help so many other parents support their sensory children.

I also need to thank the parents and teachers I have been able to work with and support at presentations and workshops along the way. It confirms the universal challenges that exist for rigid, anxious, and distracted kids, as well as pulls us all together with the common goals of acceptance and support for each other and our children.

Thank you to all the professionals out there who are working tirelessly to support all types of sensory kids and their families. Our family has been blessed to have an amazing sensory team by our side to guide, teach, and support us on our journey as individuals and as a family.

Of course, this book would not be possible without my amazing team at Touchstone Books. My editor, Michelle Howry, coached me along with great patience and expertise making the process a tremendous learning experience. To my publicist, Shida Carr, for her amazing marketing and publicity expertise, and for her energy and excitement for this project. I also need to thank my fantastic agent, Stephanie Kip Rostan, for guiding me along the way with clear direction and positive energy. To Laura Rossi Totten, my PR and social media gal extraordinaire, for intuitively understanding my message and helping me get it out to you using all possible avenues. To Mike Egan, for helping bring the book to life with his amazing photographs. To Patricia Romanowski Bashe for her copyediting and special needs expertise—her knowledge and perspective were a gift in this process. Finally, to the person who got this whole process started, I am so thankful to my friend Marnie Cochran, who heard my initial pitch and led me down a path I never would have found on my own.

Friendship takes on a new meaning when you have to listen to your friend talk about her book project nonstop, and I am so blessed to have amazing friends in my life—Amy Quadrini, Karin Duprey, Pat Bacon, Eileen Sweeney, Pam Ong, Lynn Kuzneski, Jen Reardon, Dawn Tripp, Vanessa Weiner, Lisa Rocchio, Elke Schamberg, Sue Fanning, Sybil Pierce, and Carol Aguiar: thank you! To Chanley Small and Mike Gannon, who, over lobster in Maine, were the first to listen to and enthusiastically encouraged the idea of this book.

To my mom and dad, Susan and Paul Greene, for creating a wonderfully structured and fun early environment for me growing up. The tools and lessons I learned from my parents are woven into this book in many ways. To my amazing extended family—Amy, Gregg, Bill, Kira, Ron, Kathy, Glenn, Tammy, Brian, Kate, Scott, Sarah, and all my nieces and nephews—for being such an important part of my family's love and connection to life.

And last but certainly not least, for my amazing family to whom this book is dedicated. To Ian and Ella for teaching me how to be the best possible person and parent I can be, and to my husband, Ron, for seeing and believing in me things I was not yet able to see and believe in myself.

Index

Note: Page numbers in *italics* refer to illustrations

About the Author

CAROLYN DALGLIESH spent eleven years in sales, customer service management, and executive recruitment, with both small businesses and Fortune 500 companies, before shifting her focus to raising her two small children. Carolyn's professional experience and personal journey as a sensory parent fueled her interest in organizing, and led her to recognize how good systems contribute not only to career success but also to personal well-being.

Carolyn founded Systems for Sensory Kids, LLC, a leading-edge organizing model that bridges the gap between clinical support and practical in-home solutions for rigid, anxious, and distracted kids. In addition to her sensory organizing work with families, she has published numerous articles and presents regularly at conferences for parents, caregivers, and educators.

A member of the National Association of Professional Organizers (NAPO), Carolyn is also the president of Simple Organizing Strategies, a professional organizing service for home and small business. She lives in Rhode Island with her husband and two children. Visit her at thesensorychildgetsorganized.com.

Logan-Hocking Co. District Library
230 East Main Street
Logan, Ohio 43138